Color Test

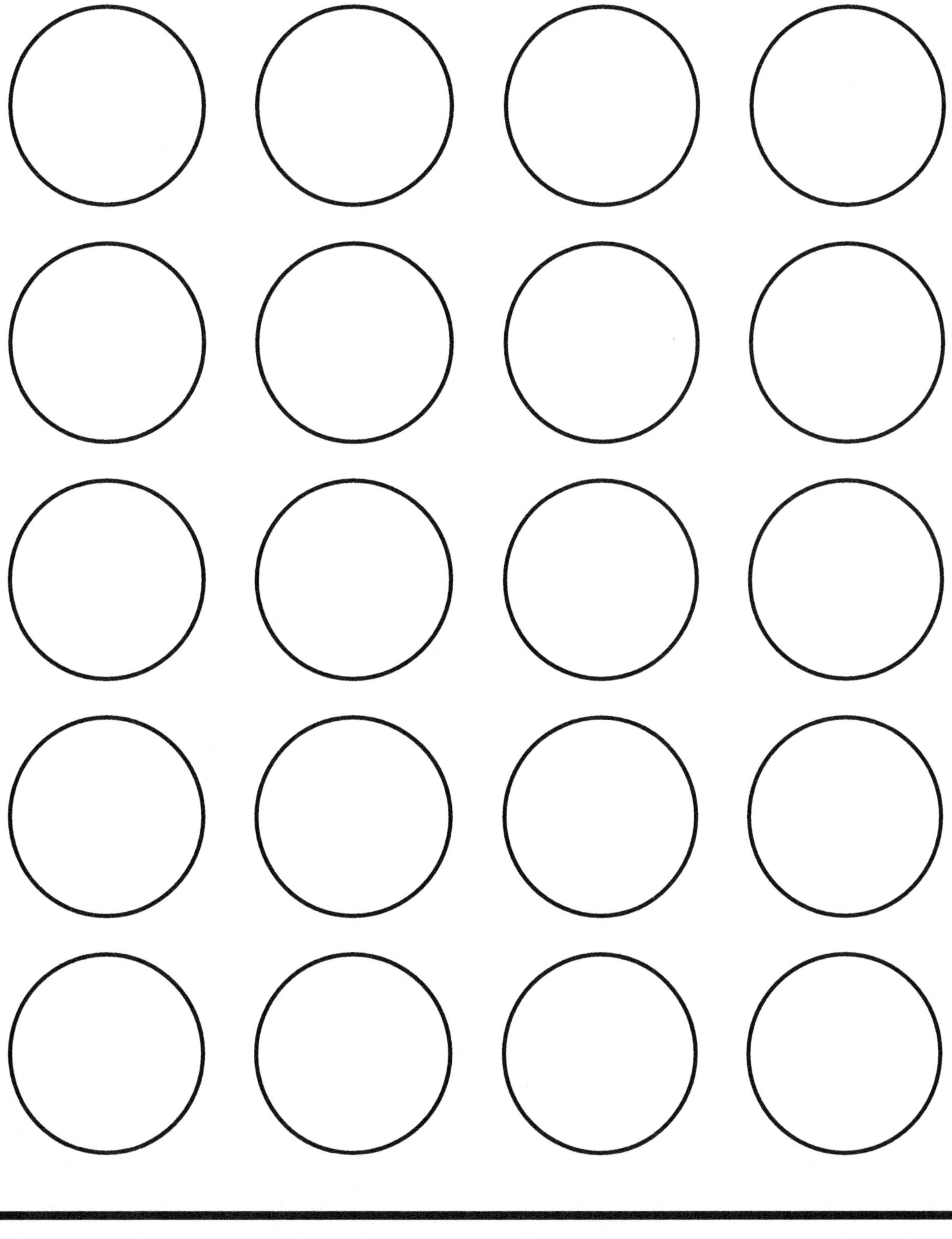

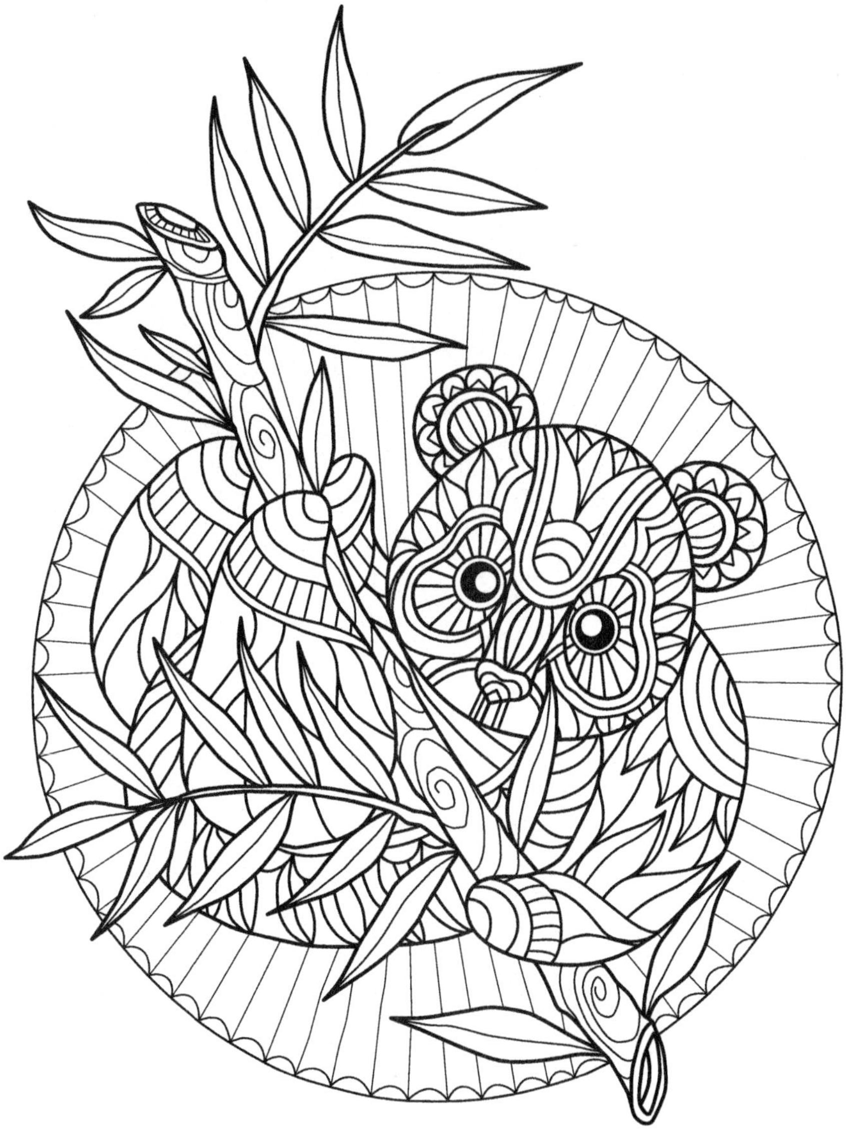

This Book Belongs To:

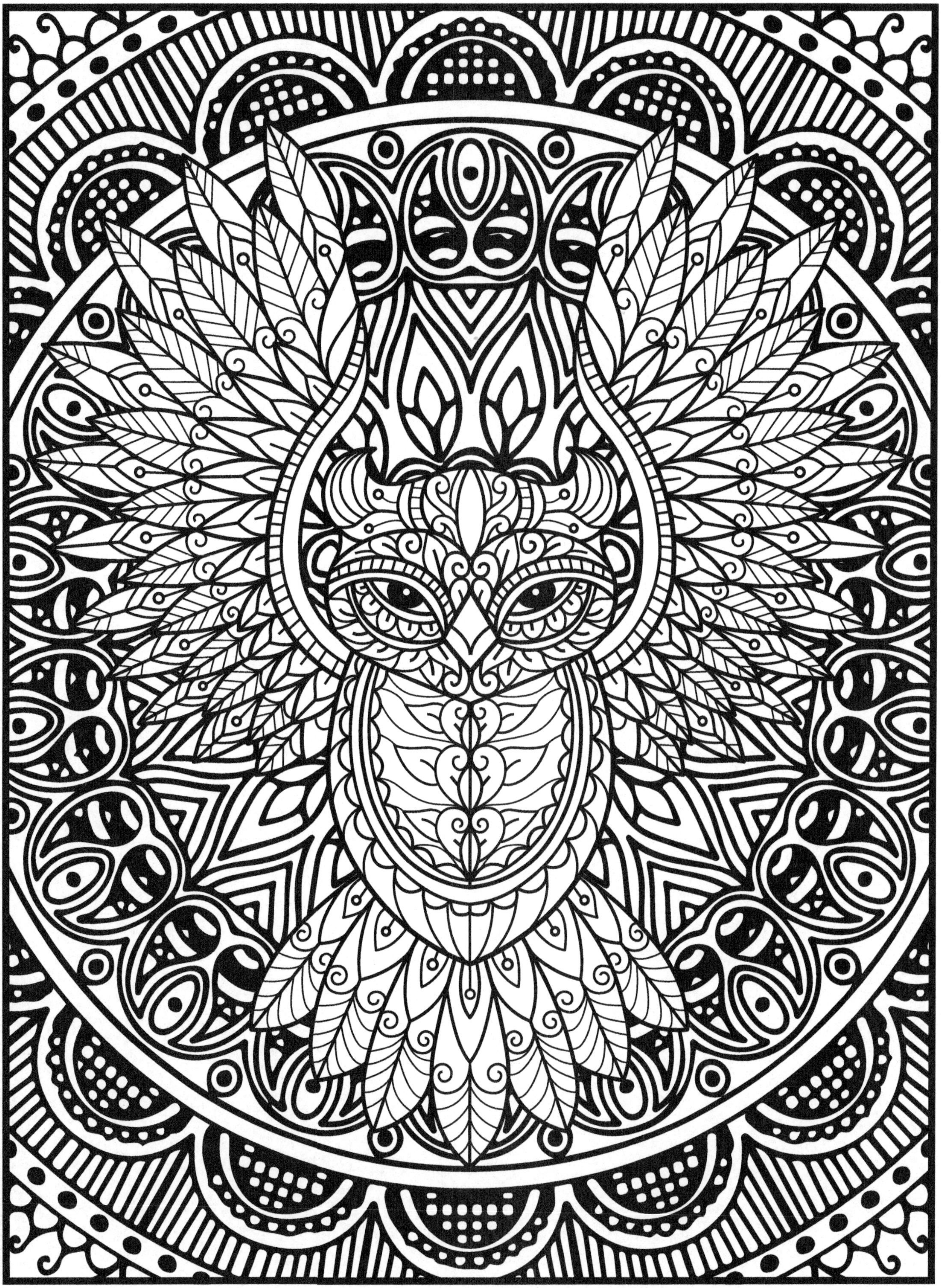

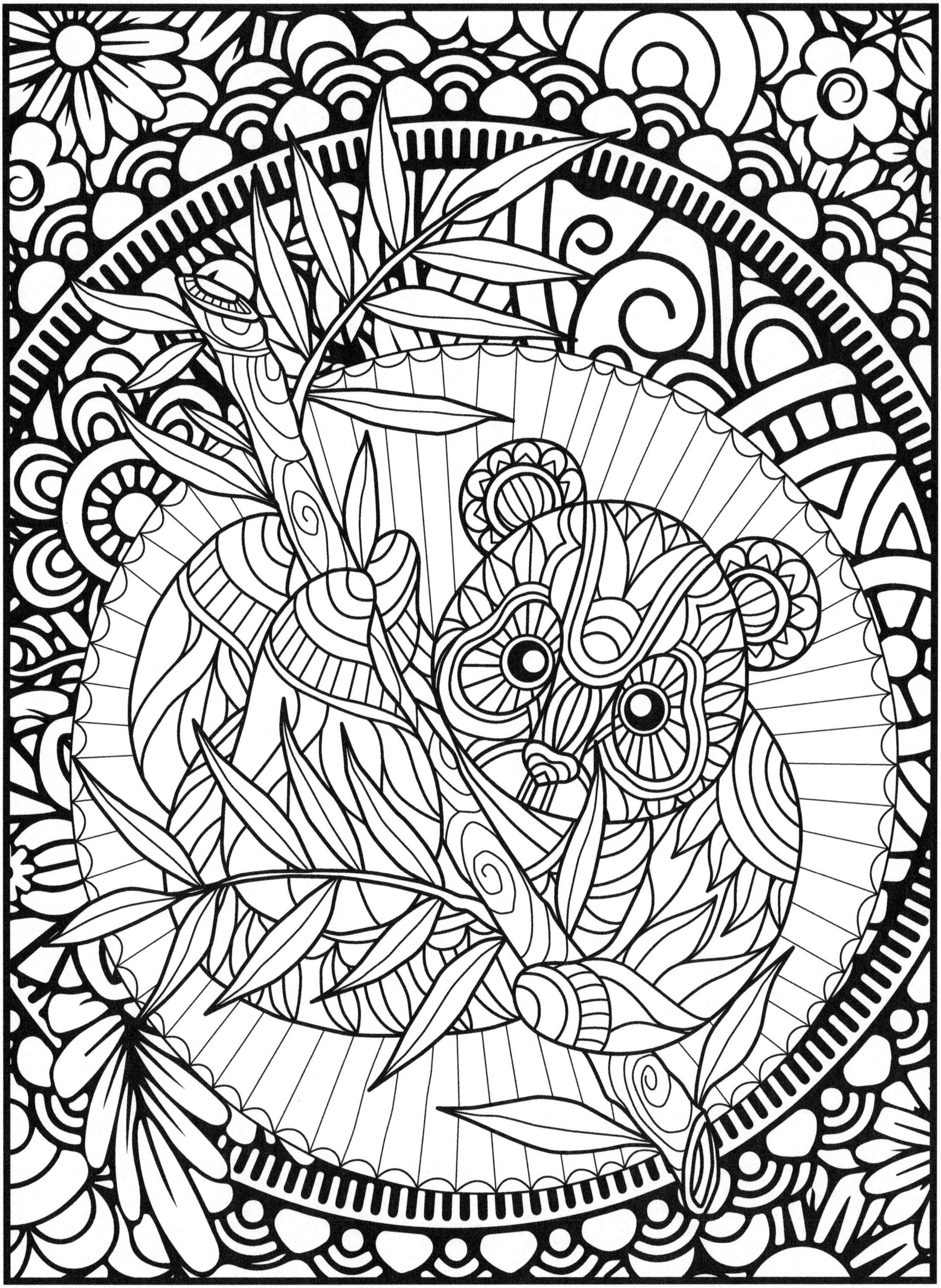

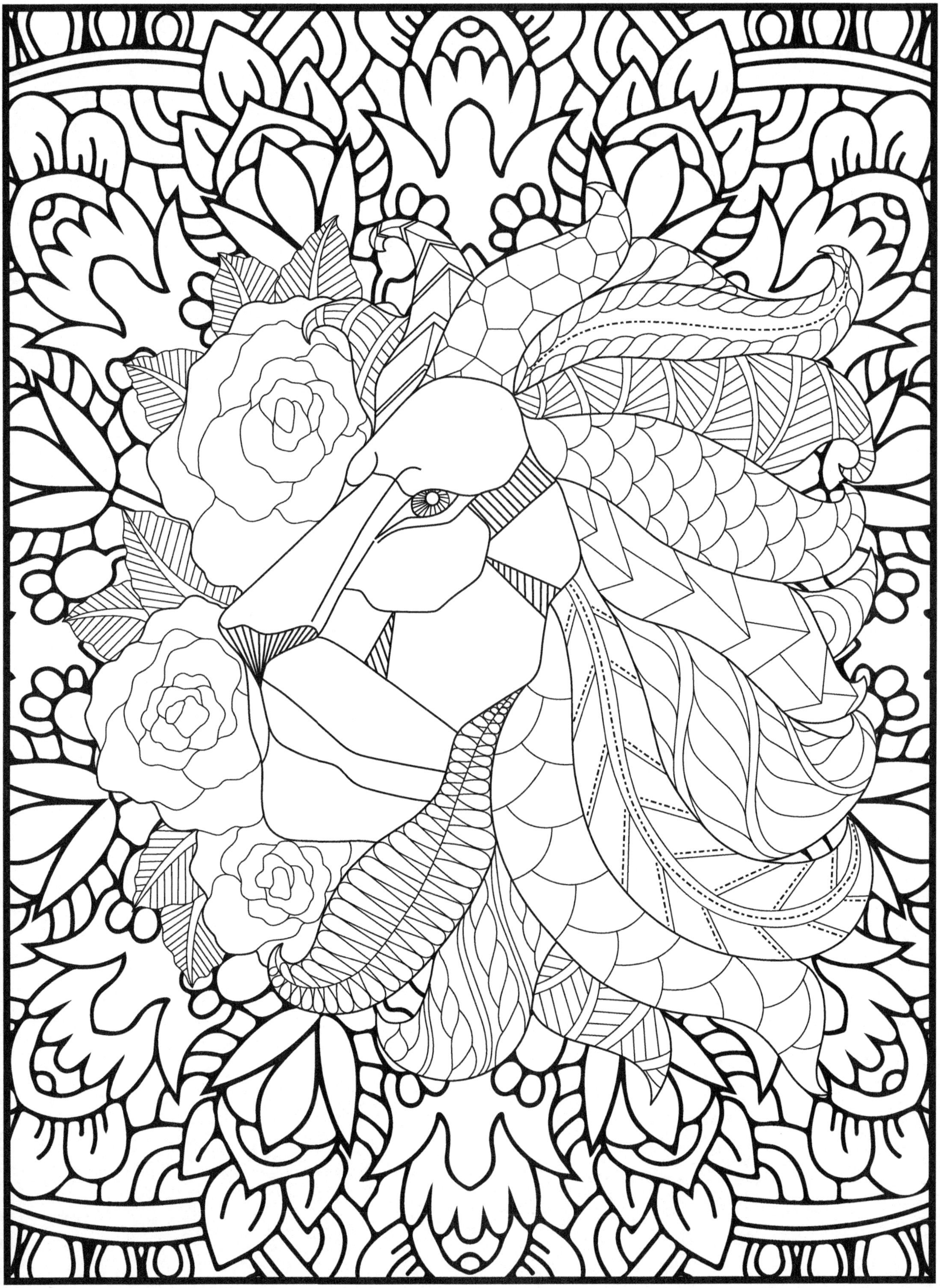

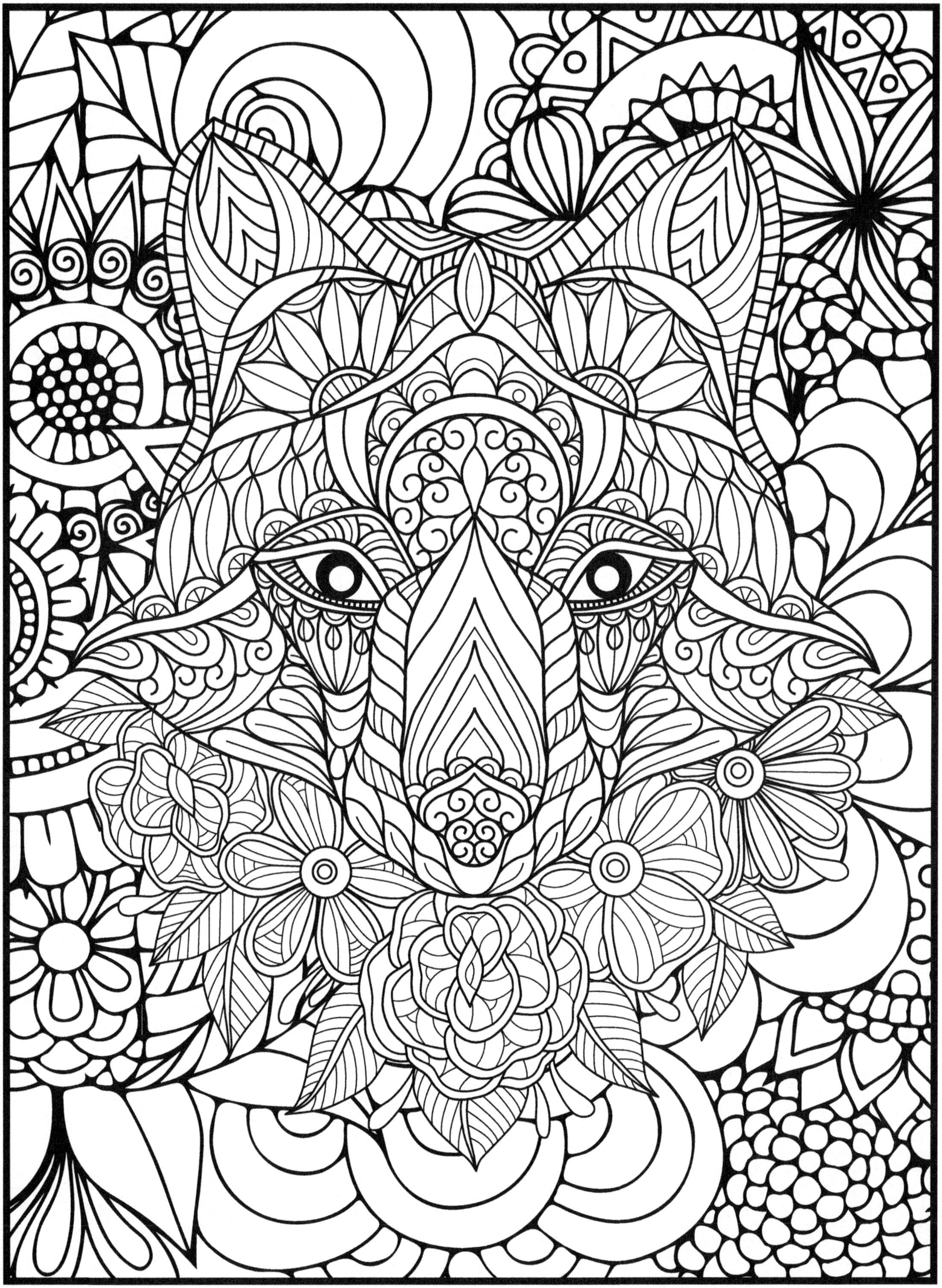

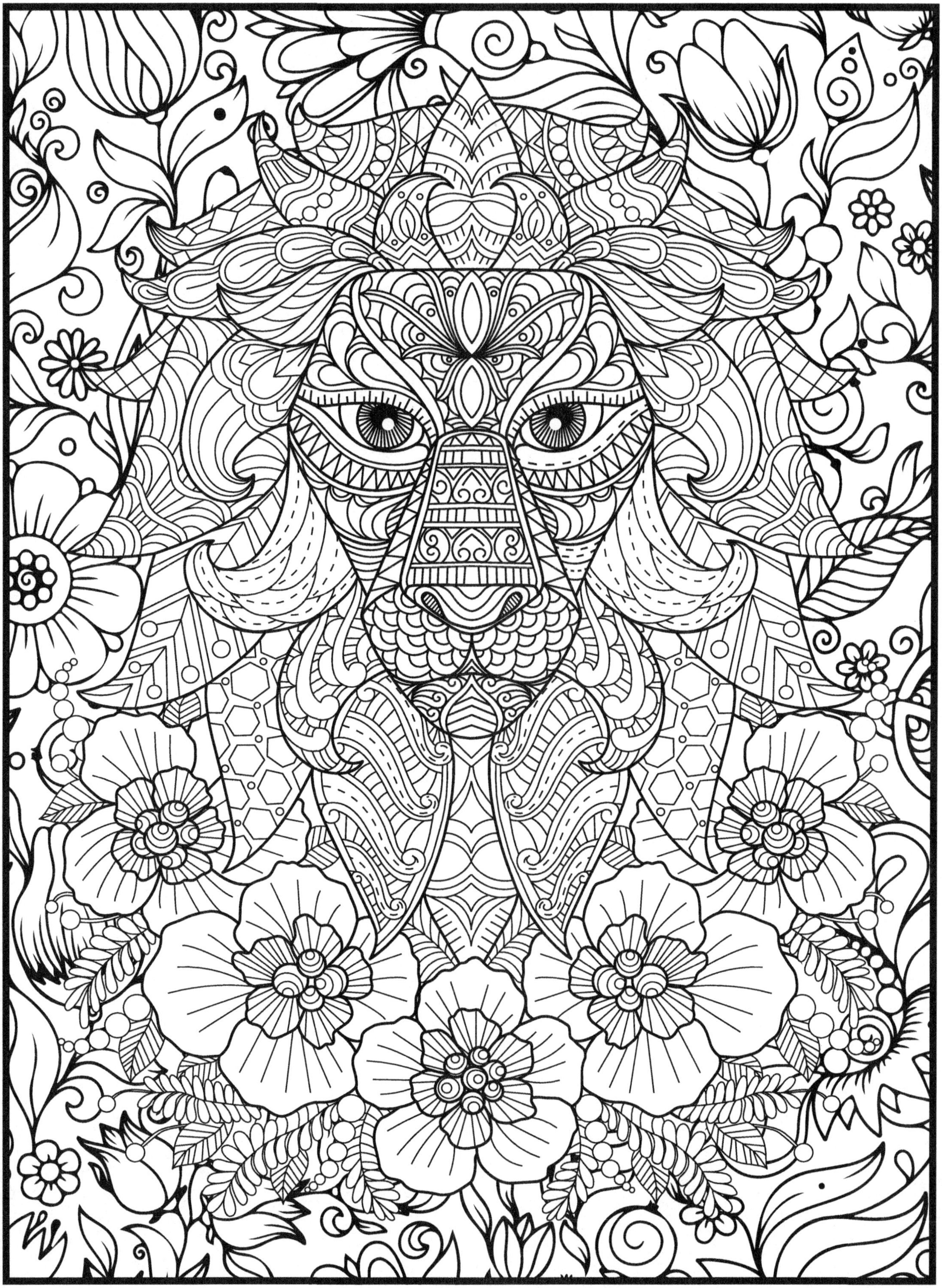

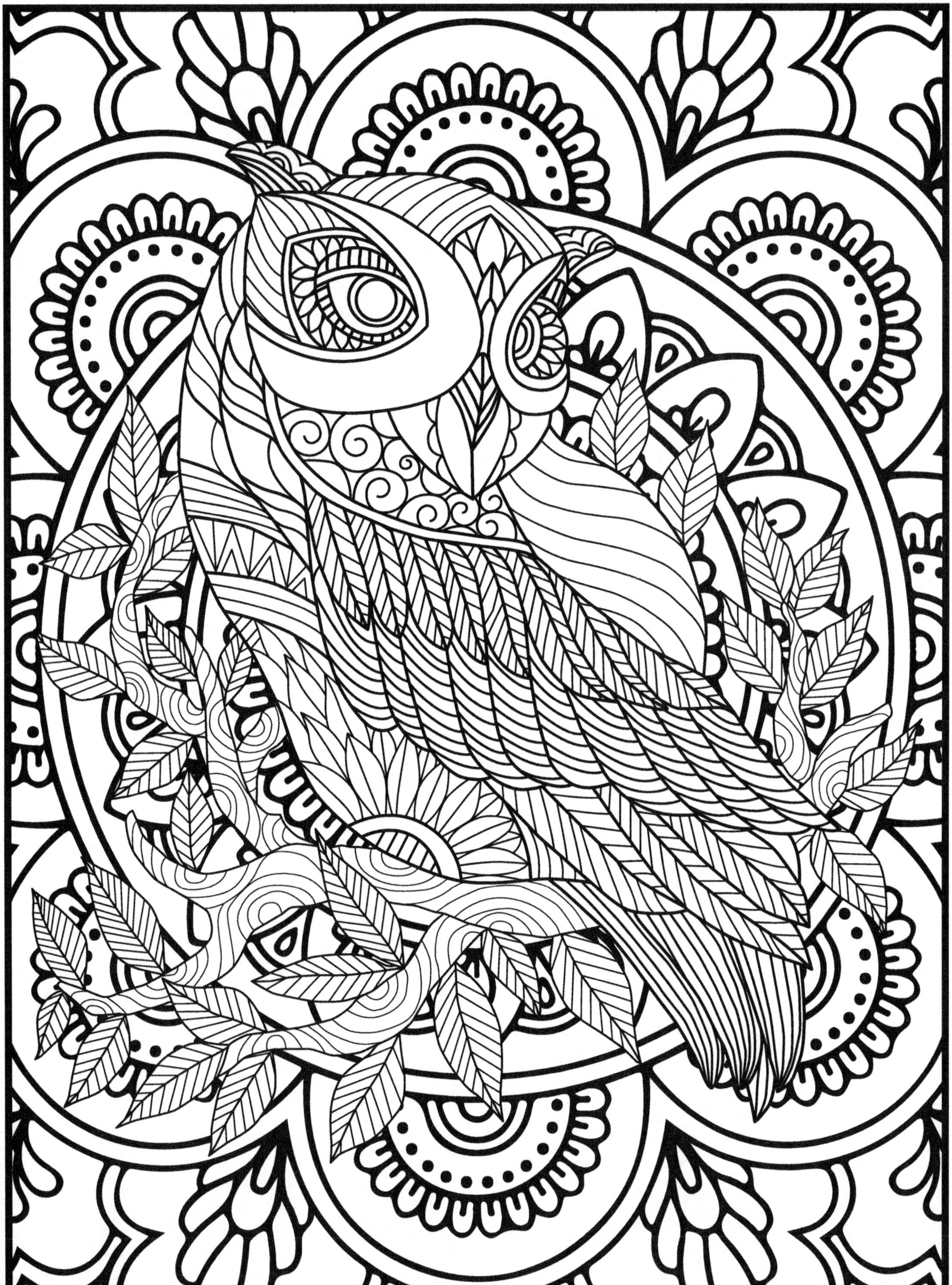

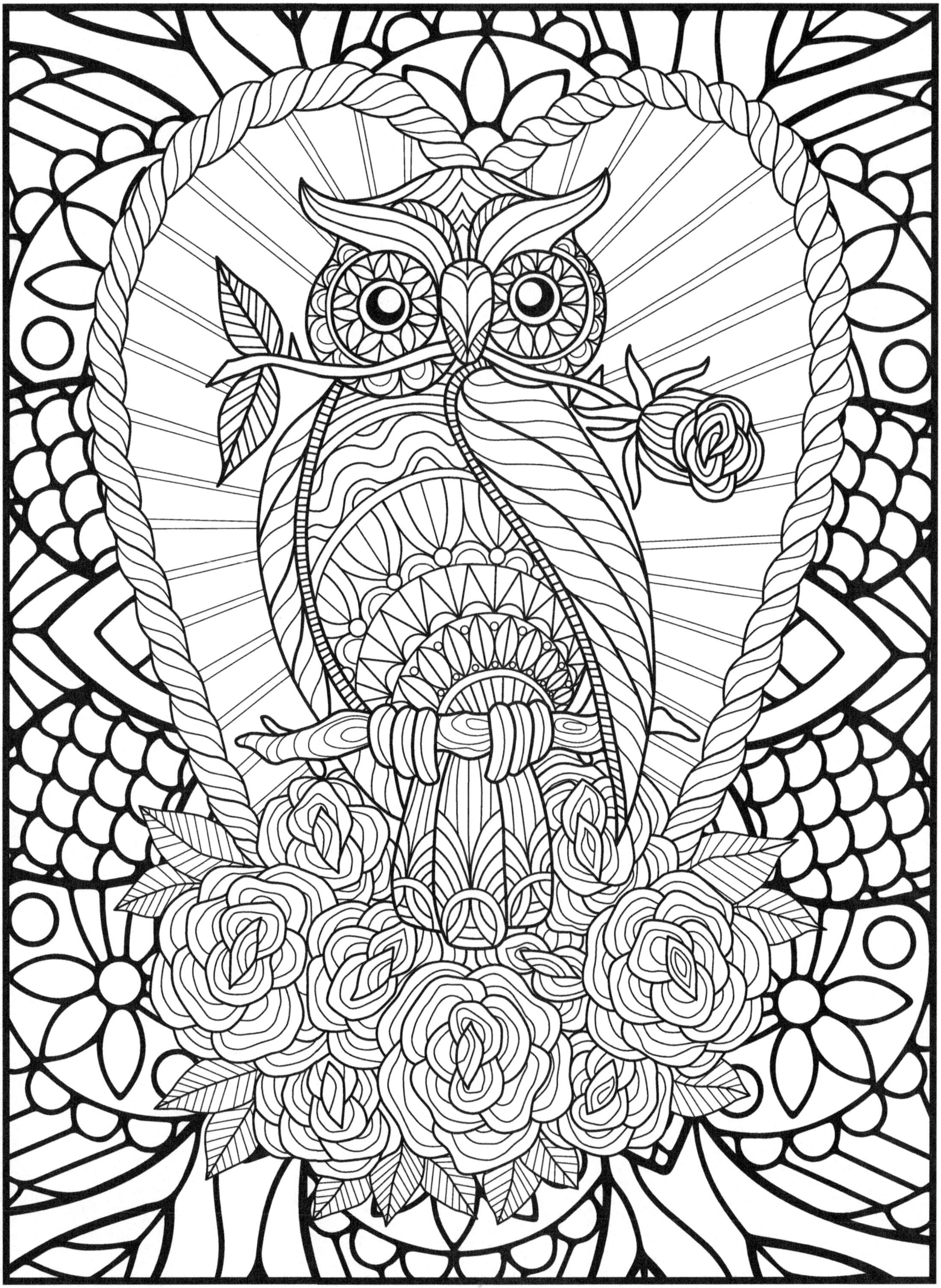

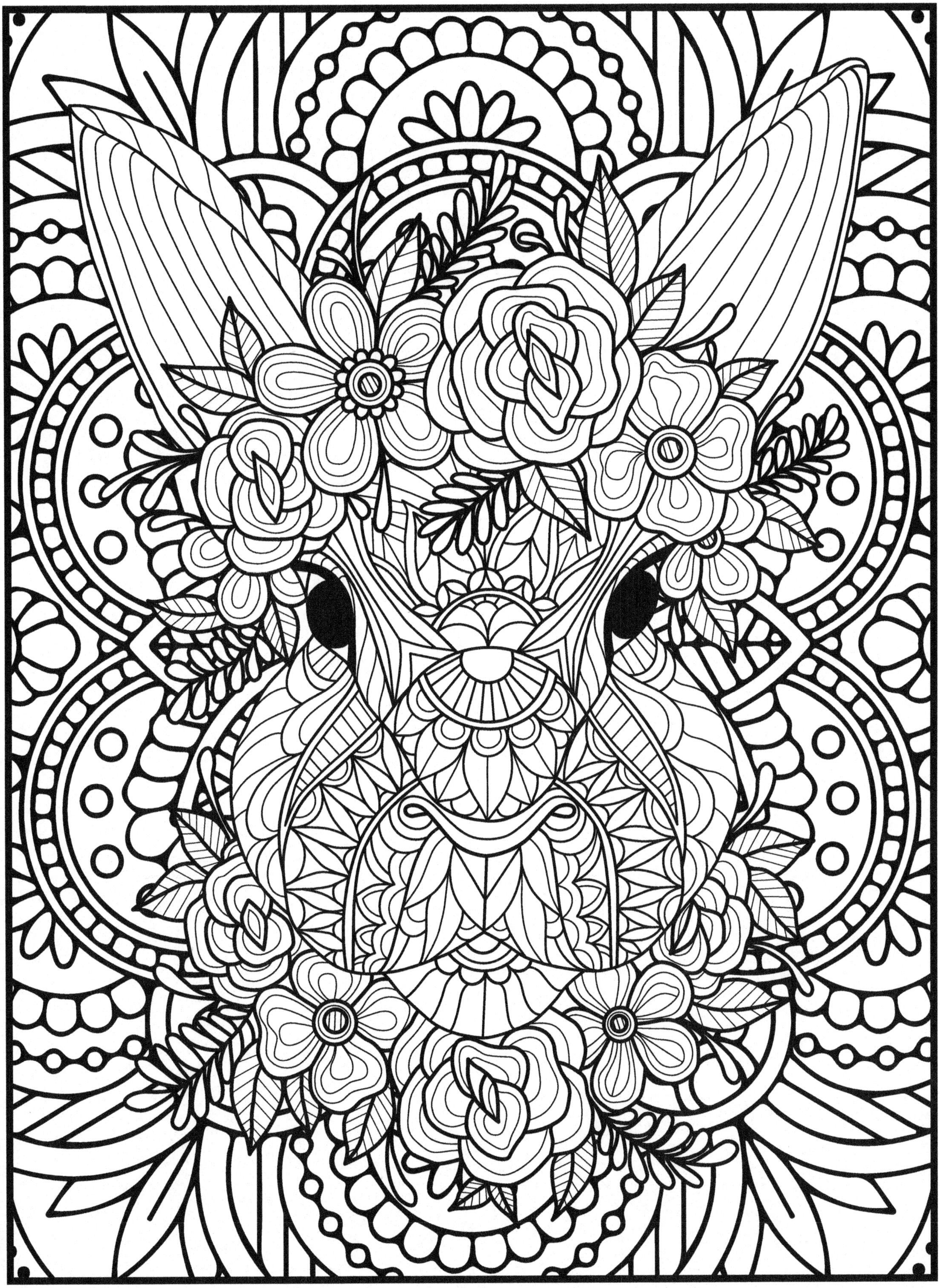

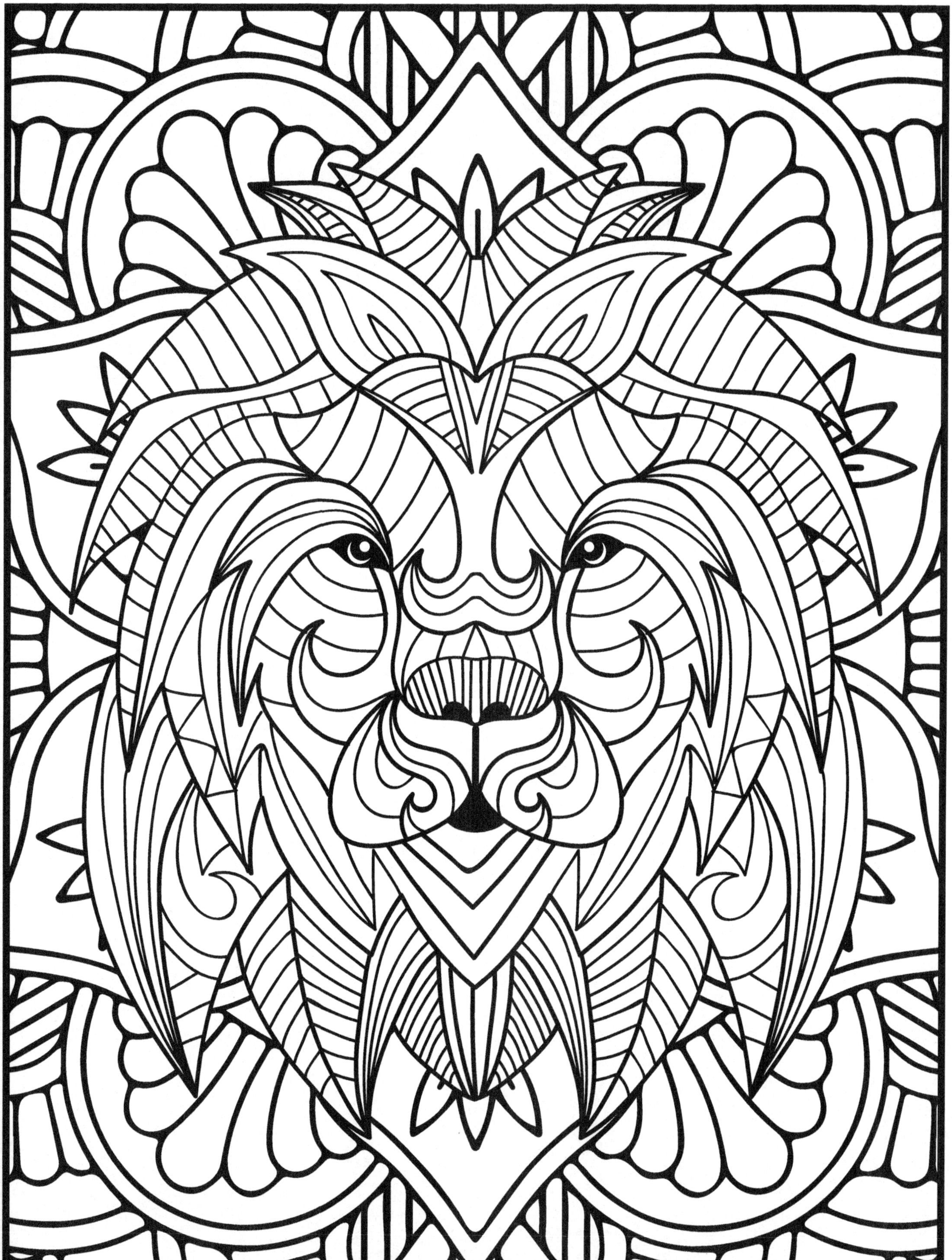

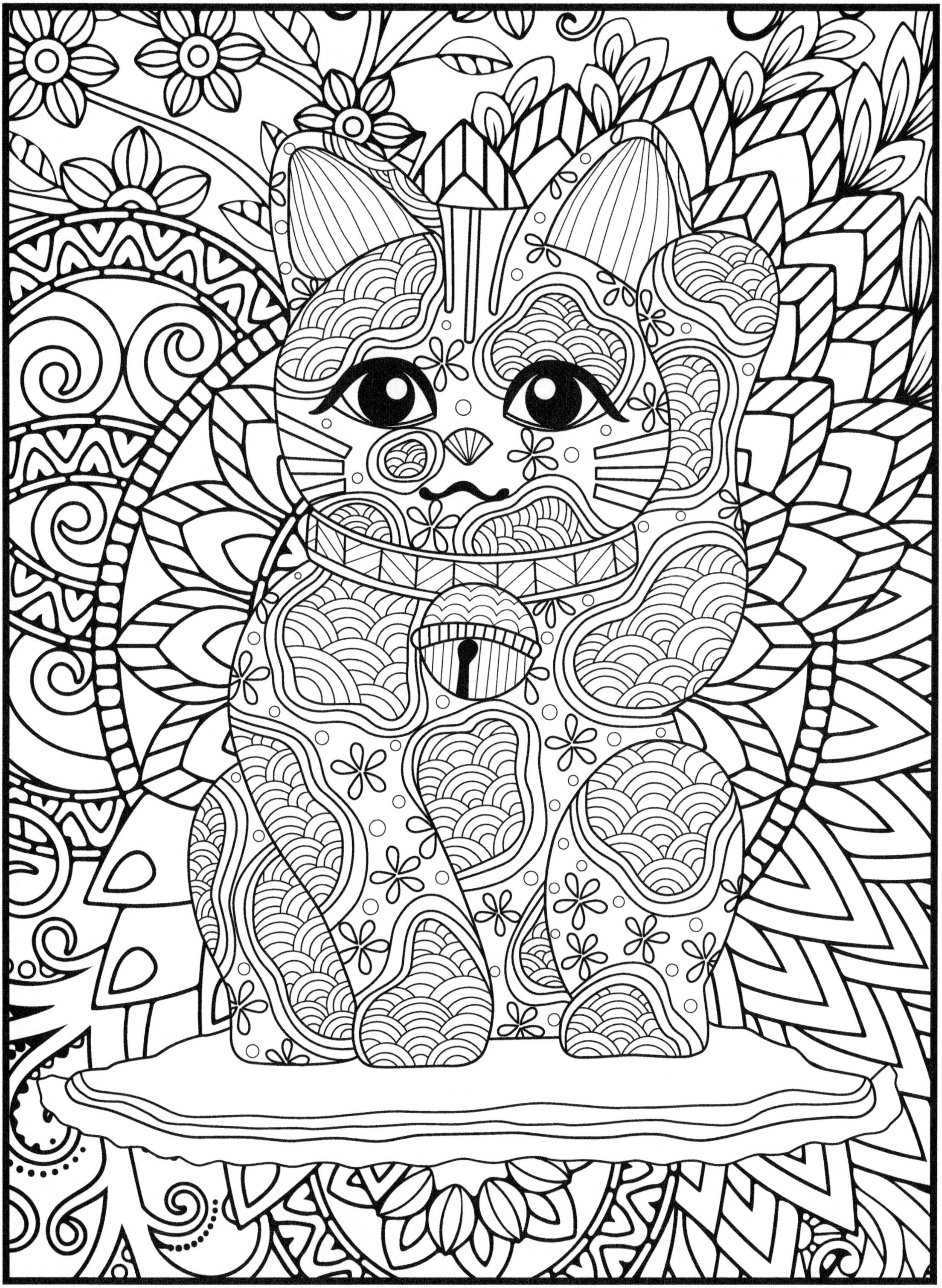

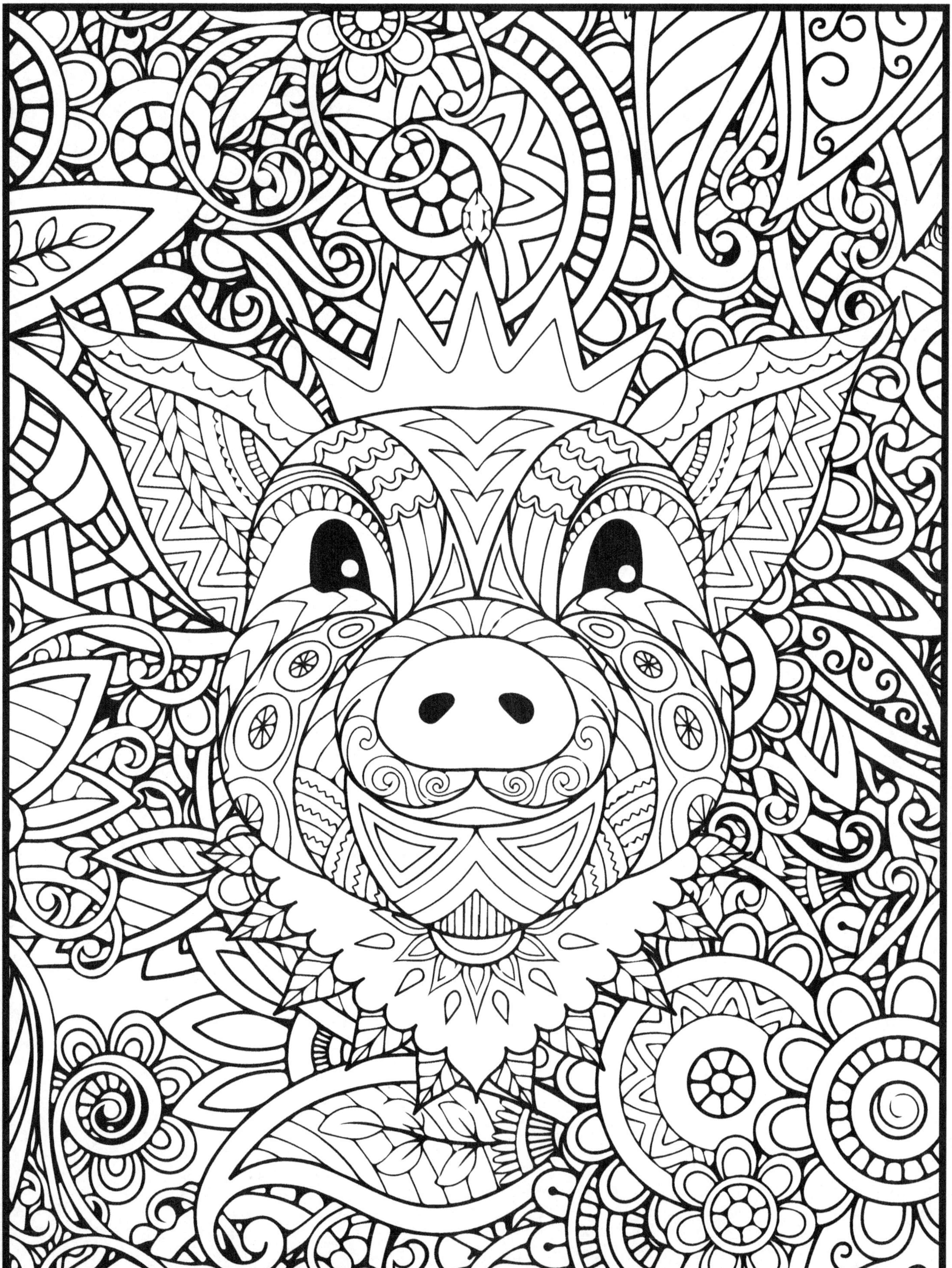

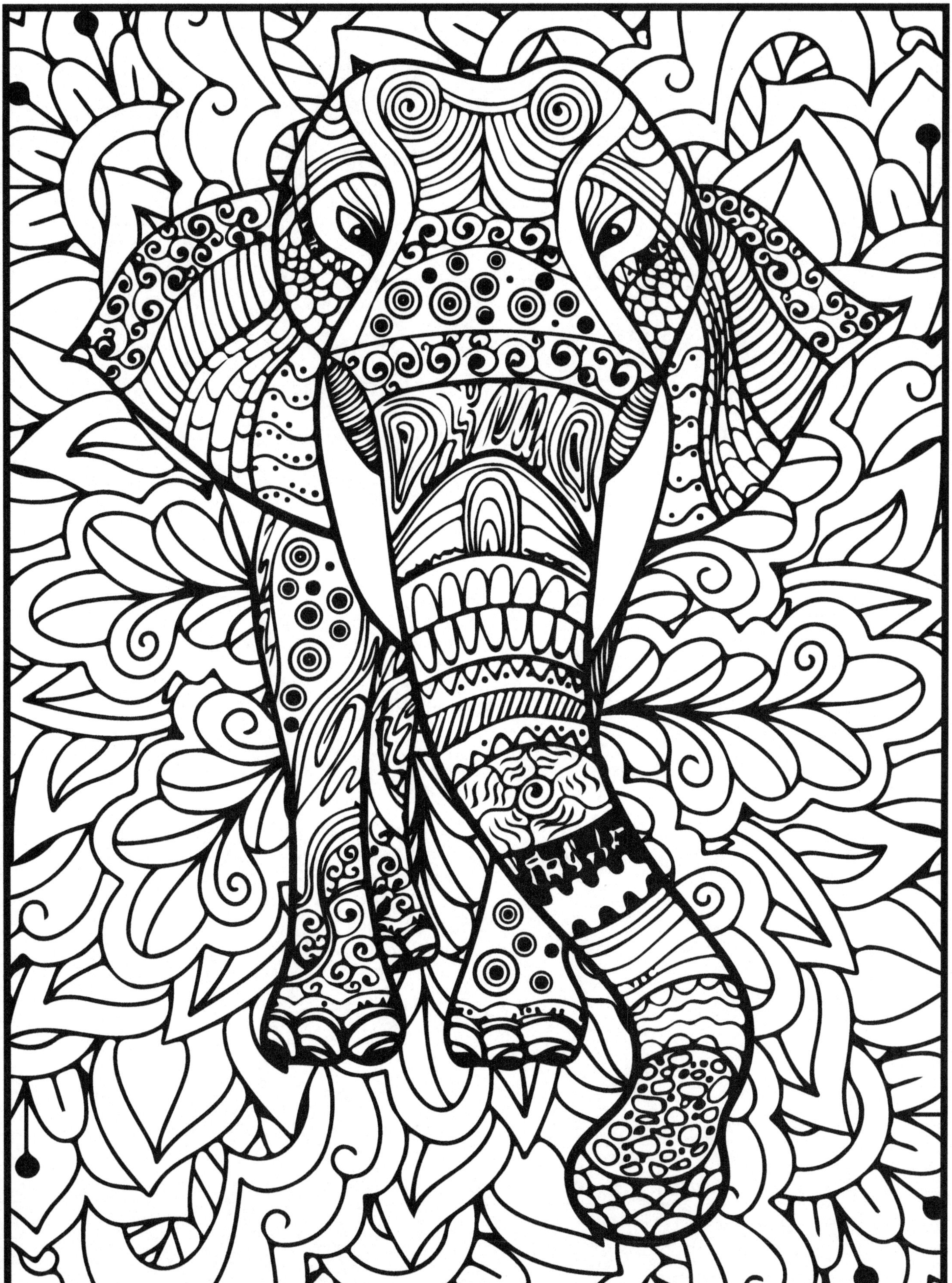

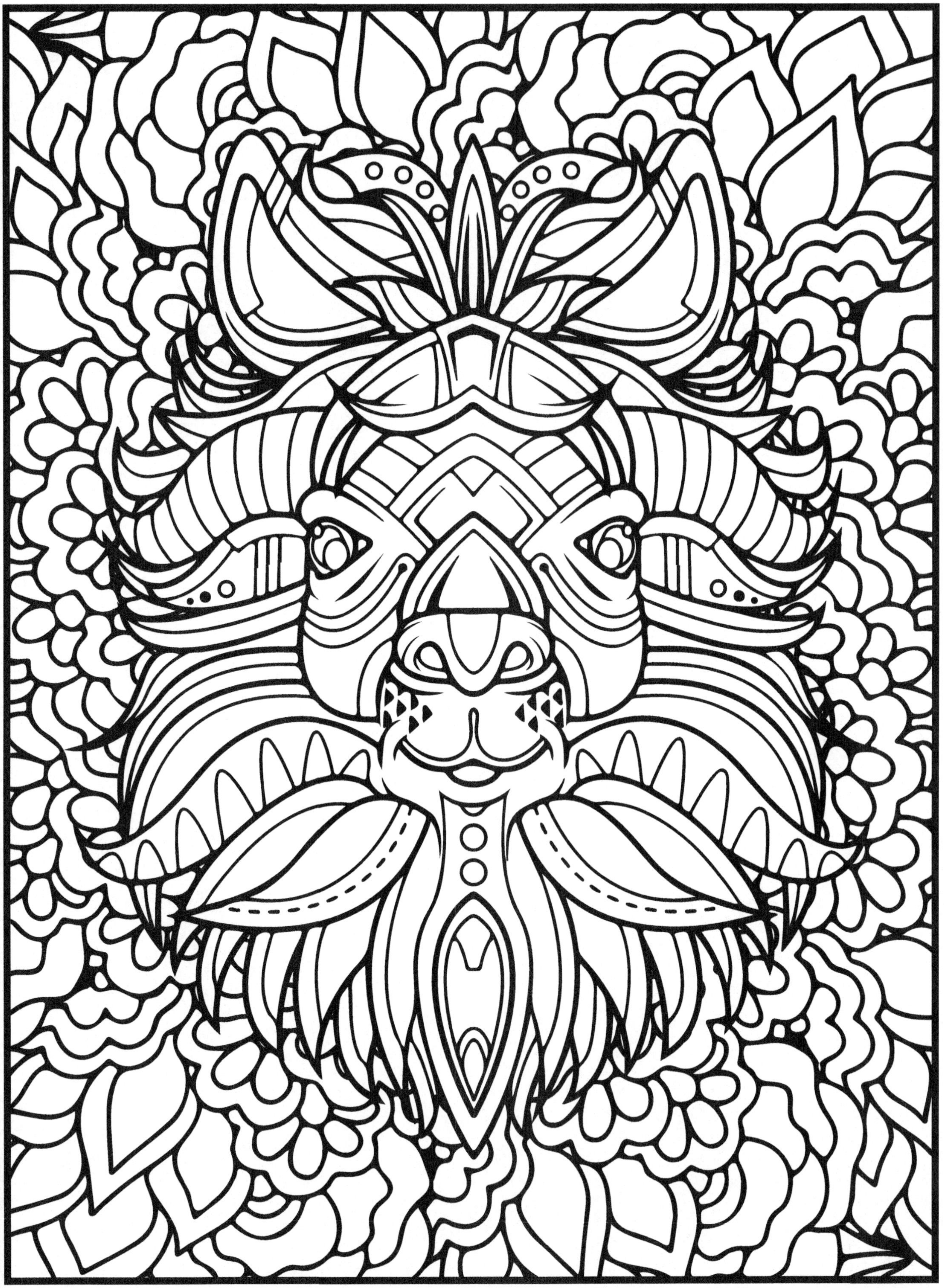

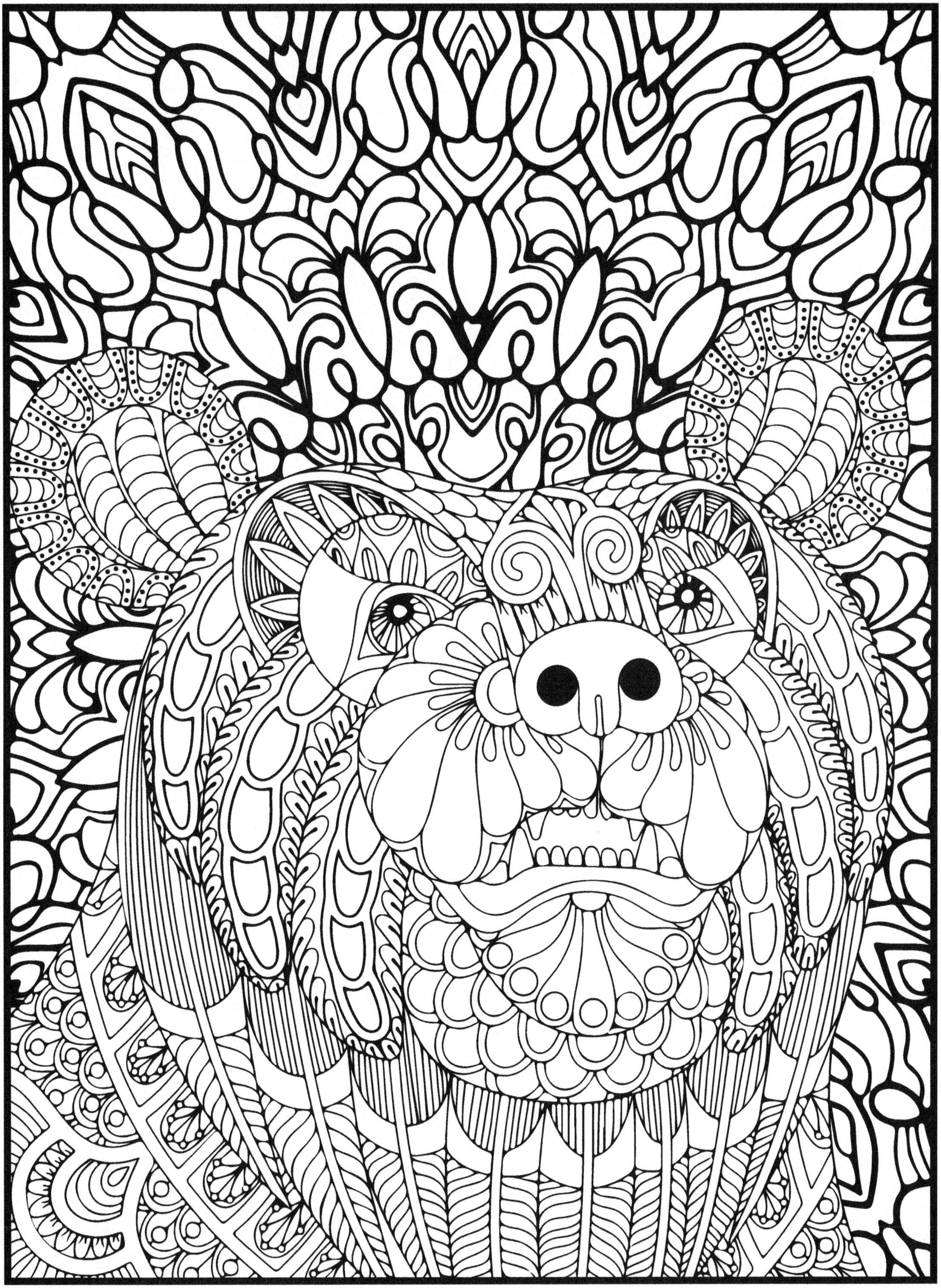

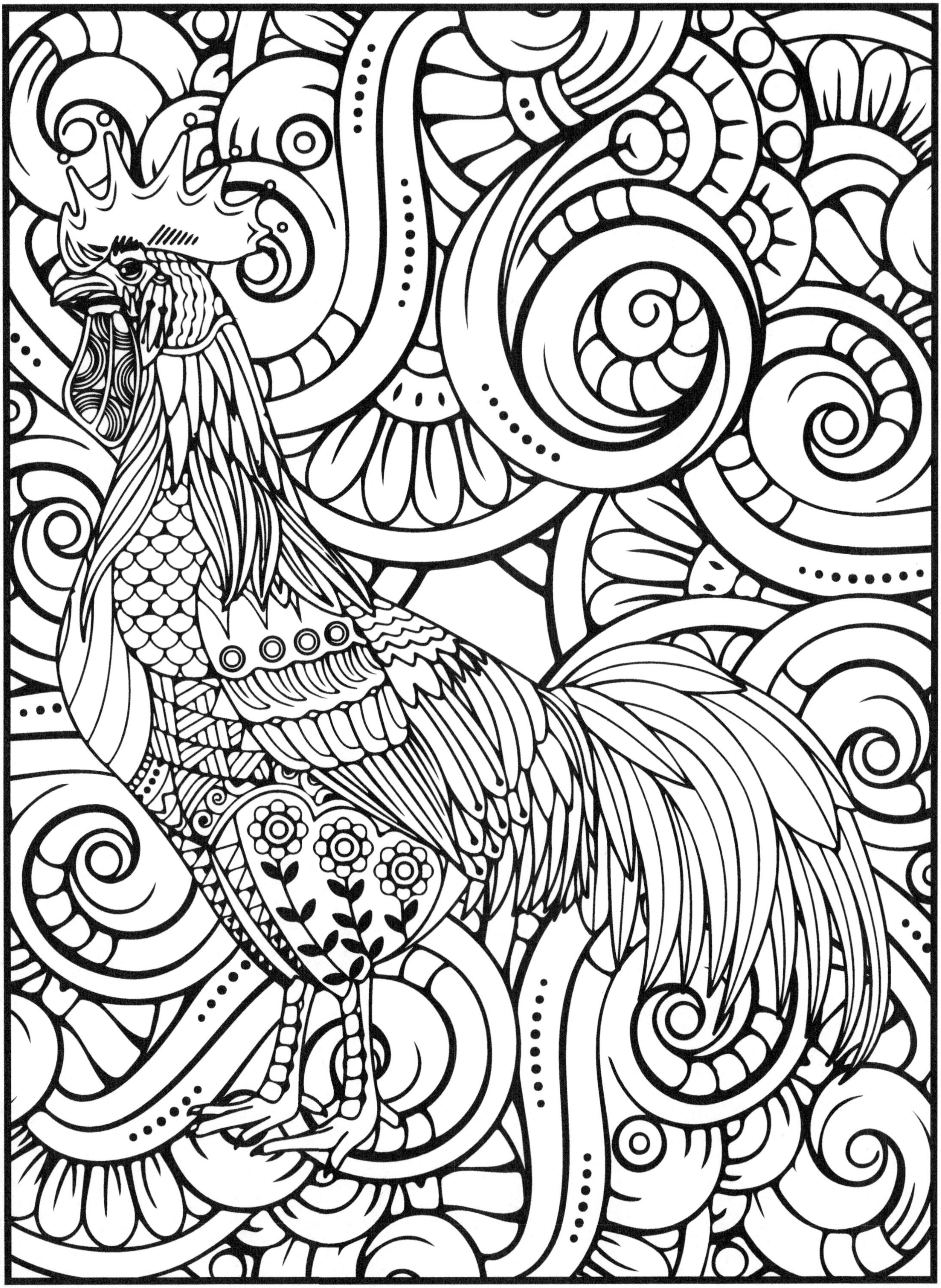

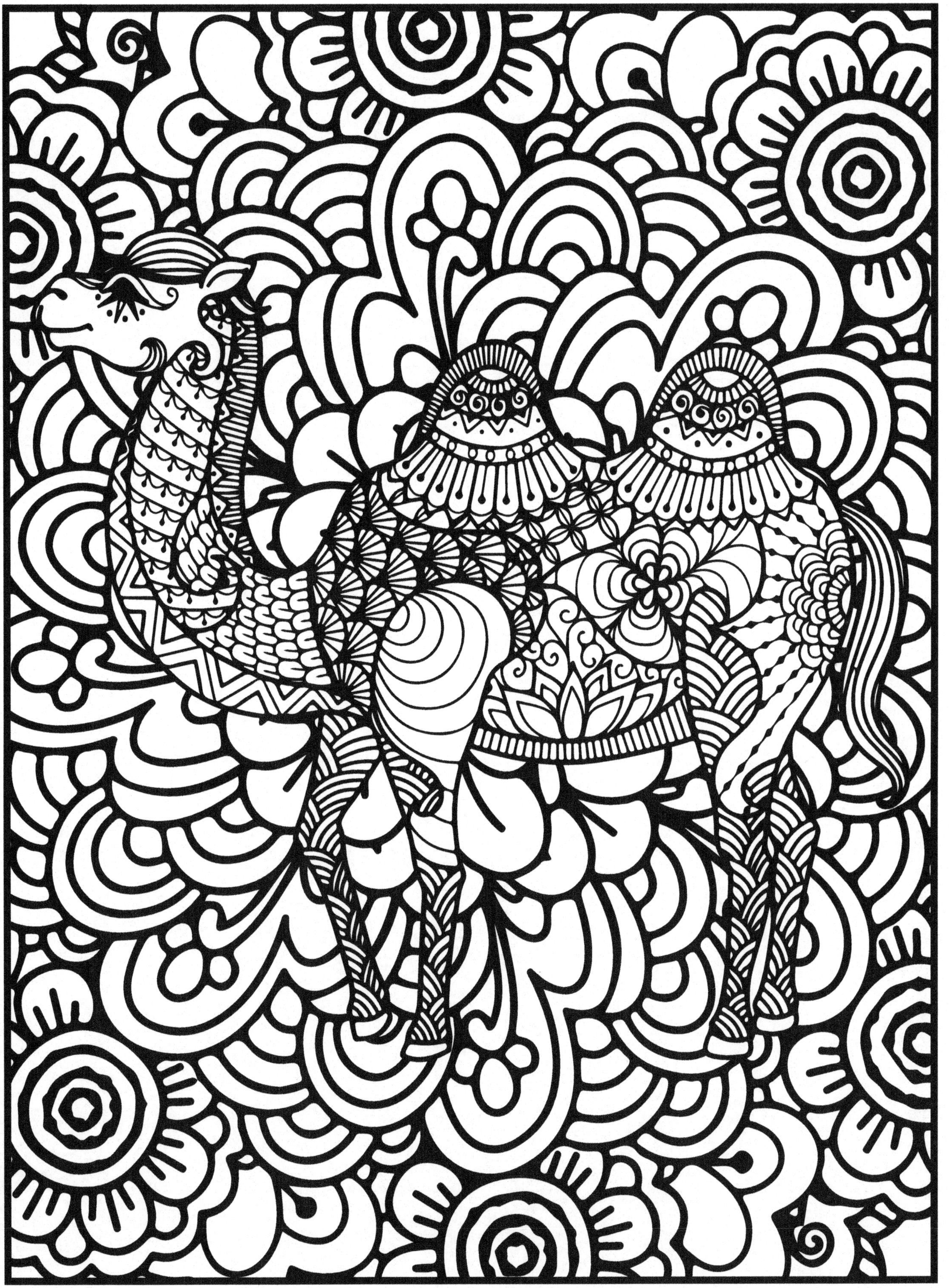

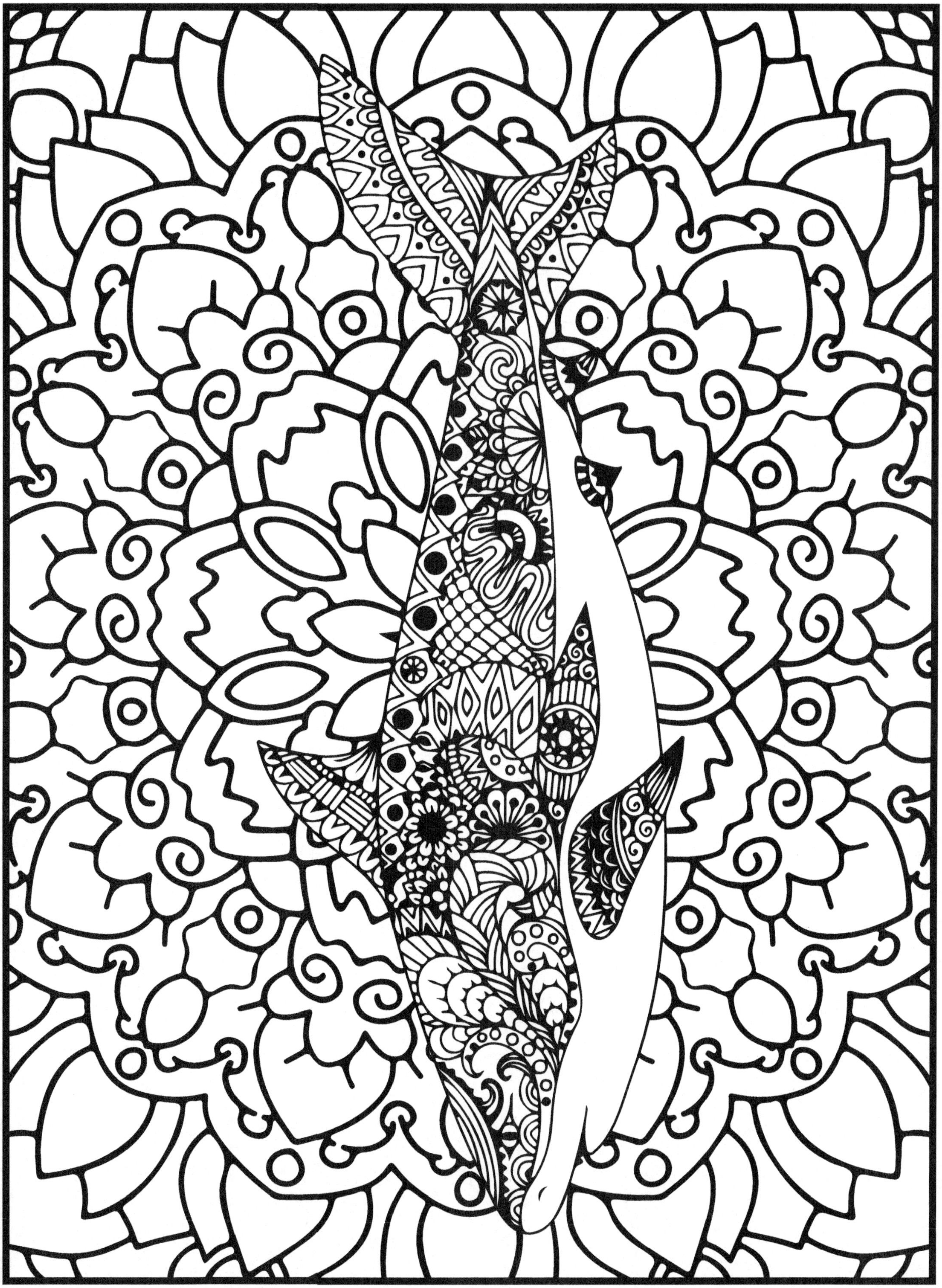

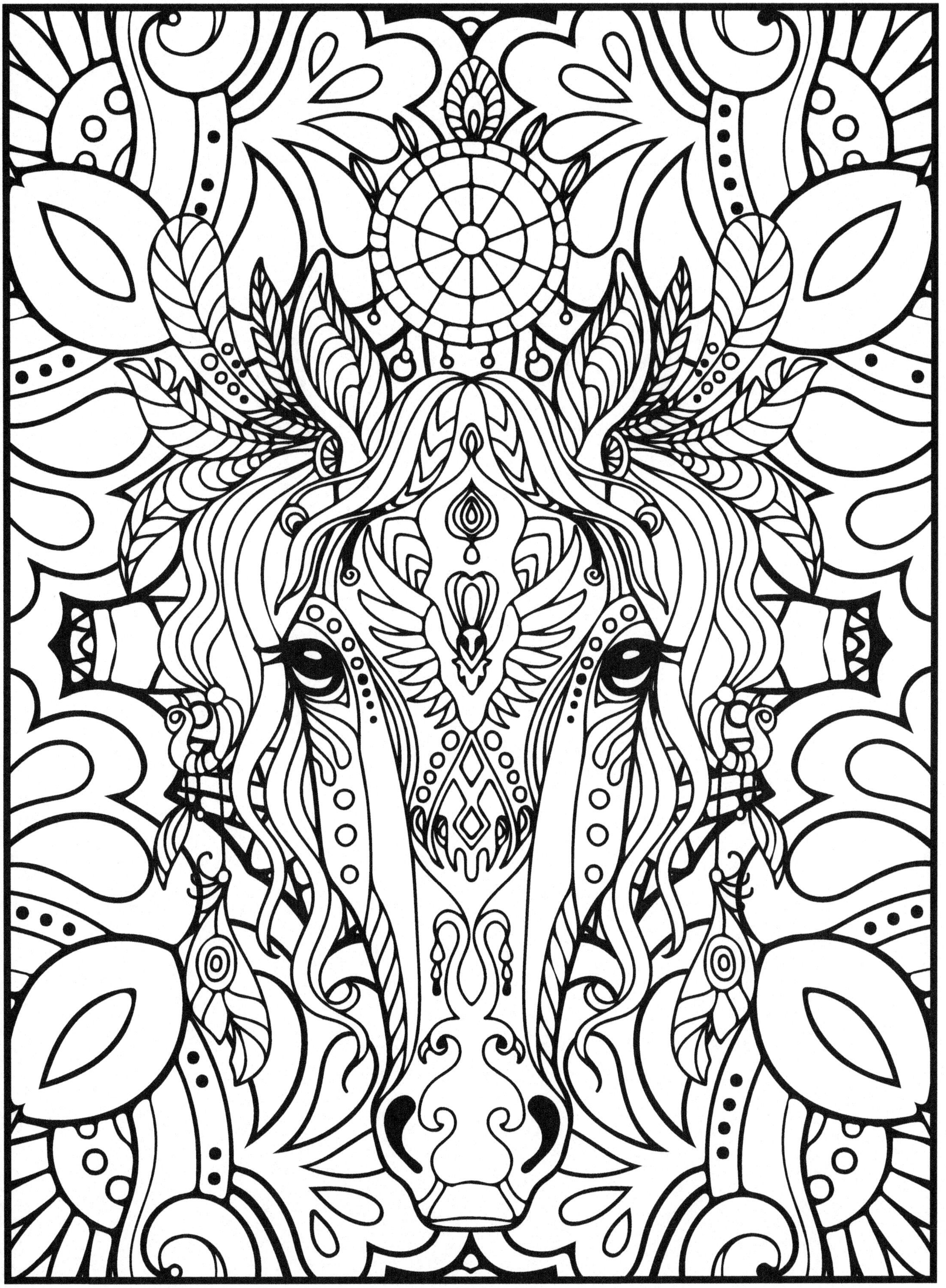

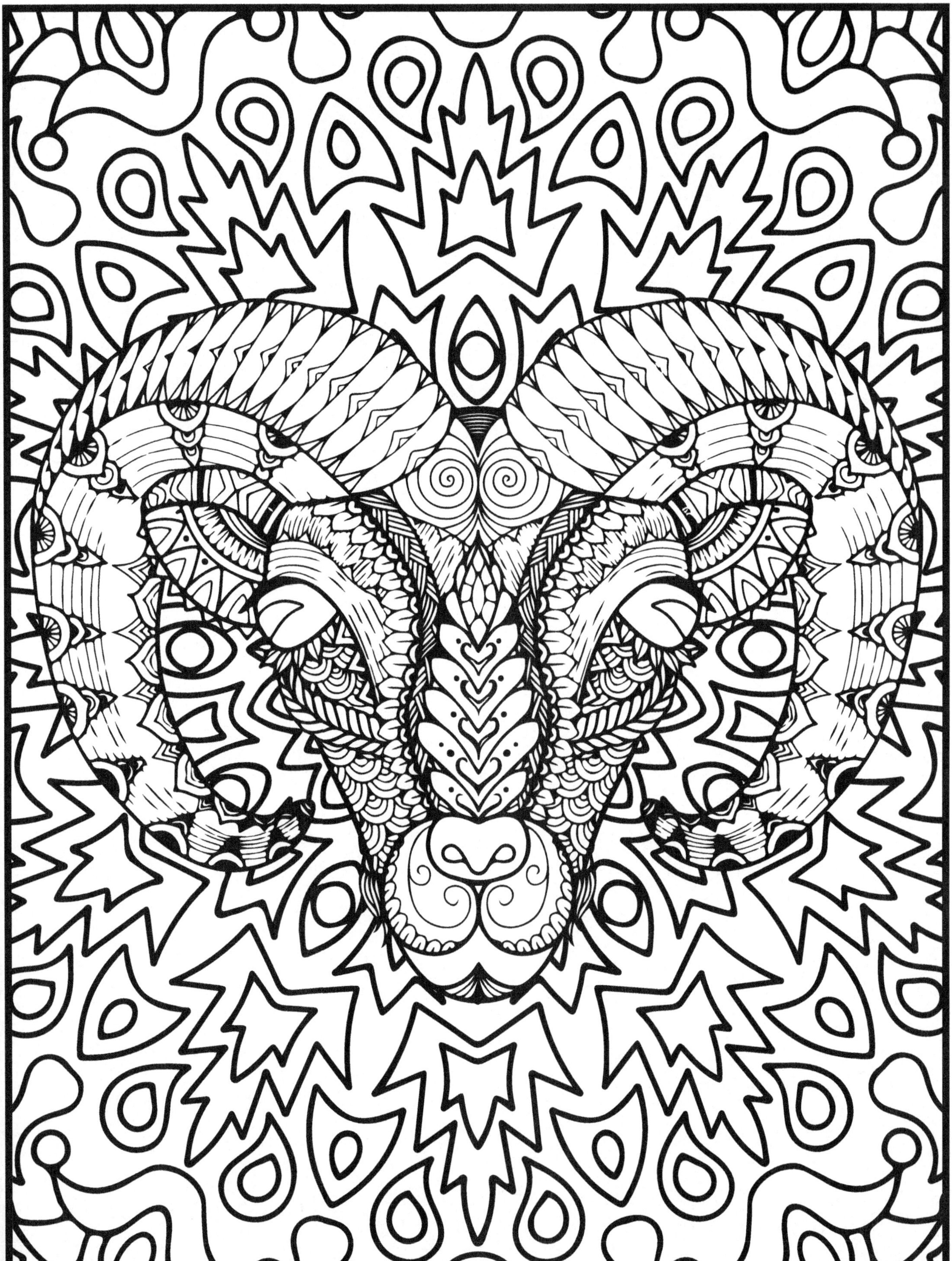

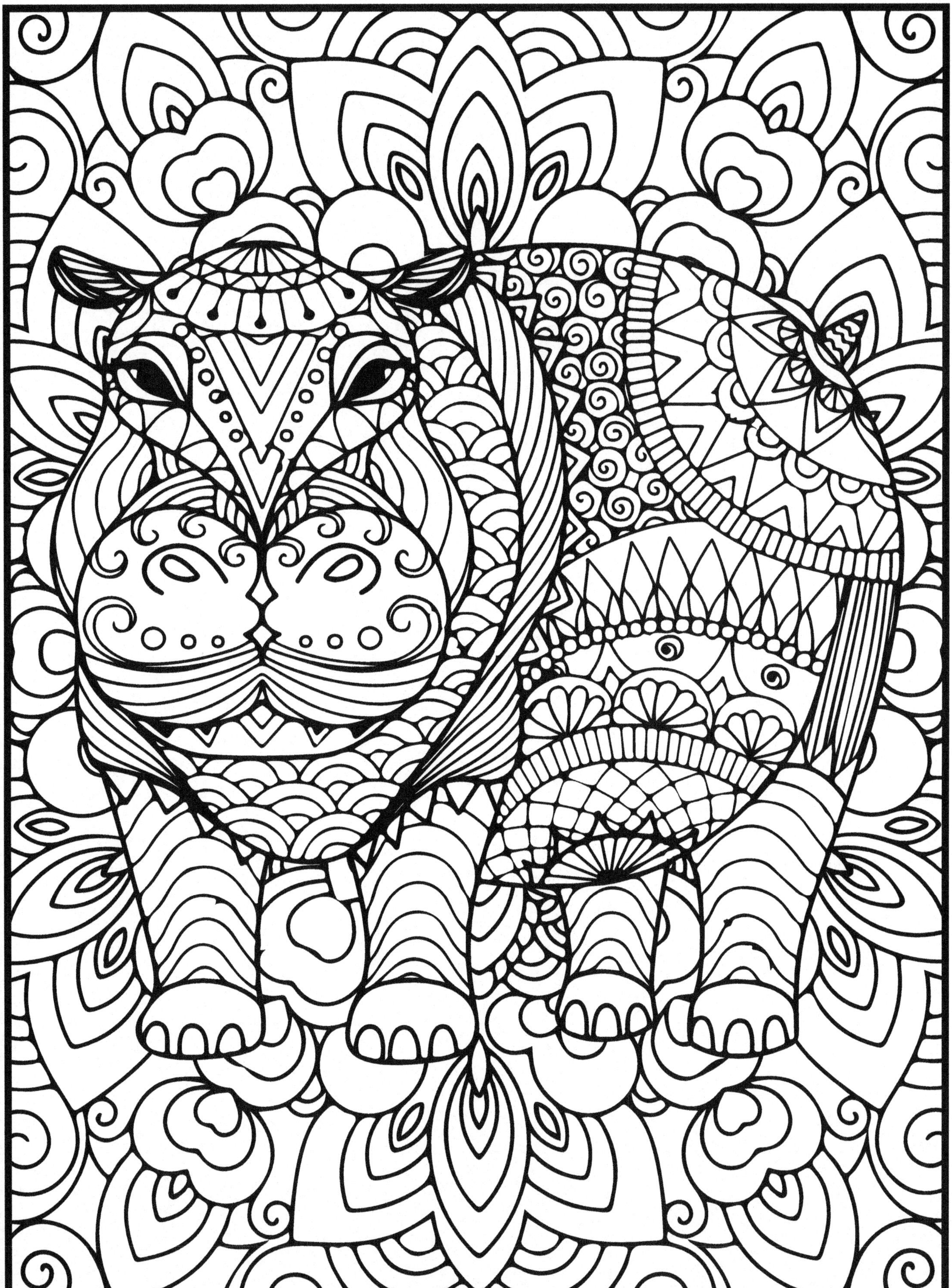

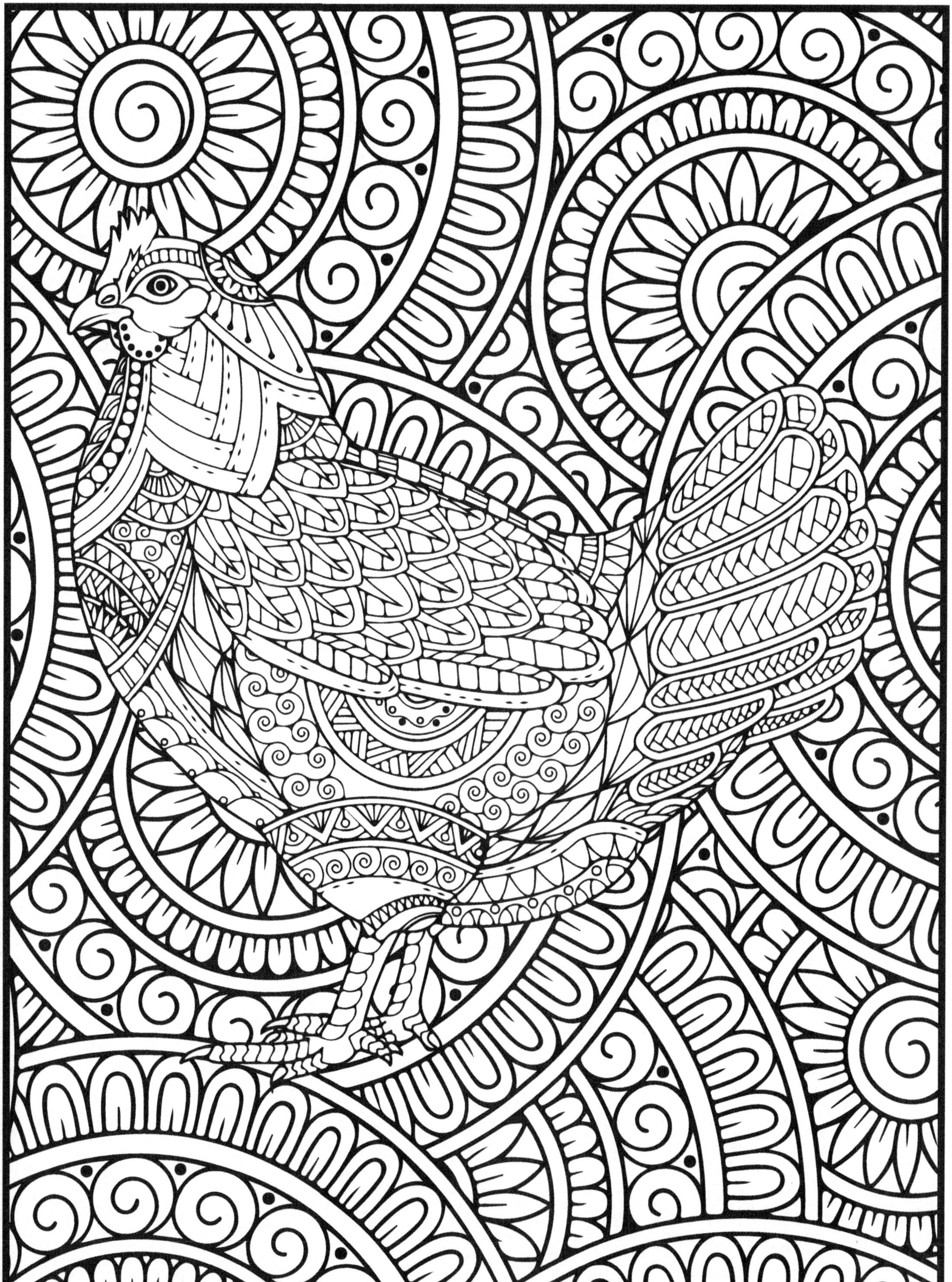

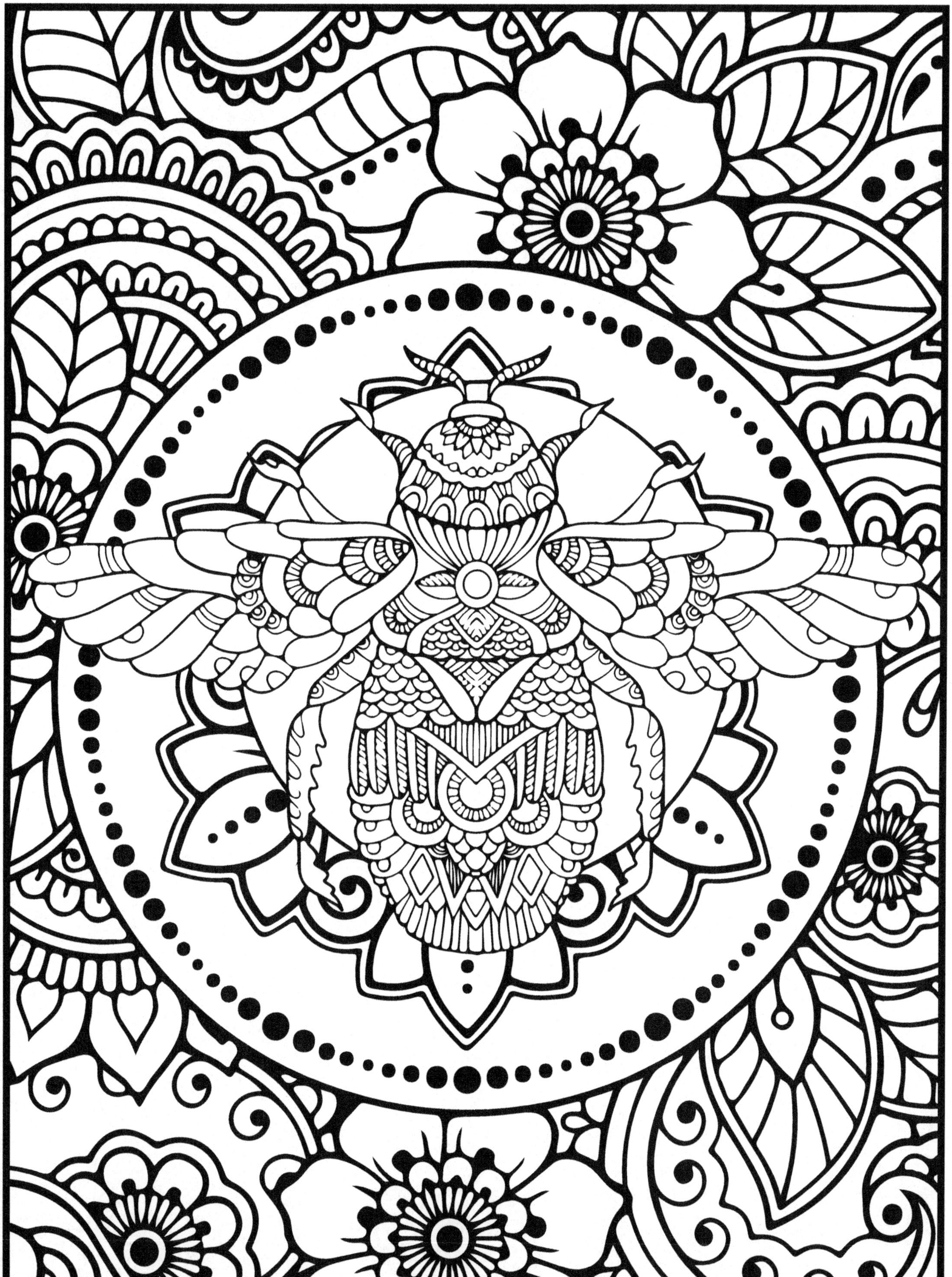

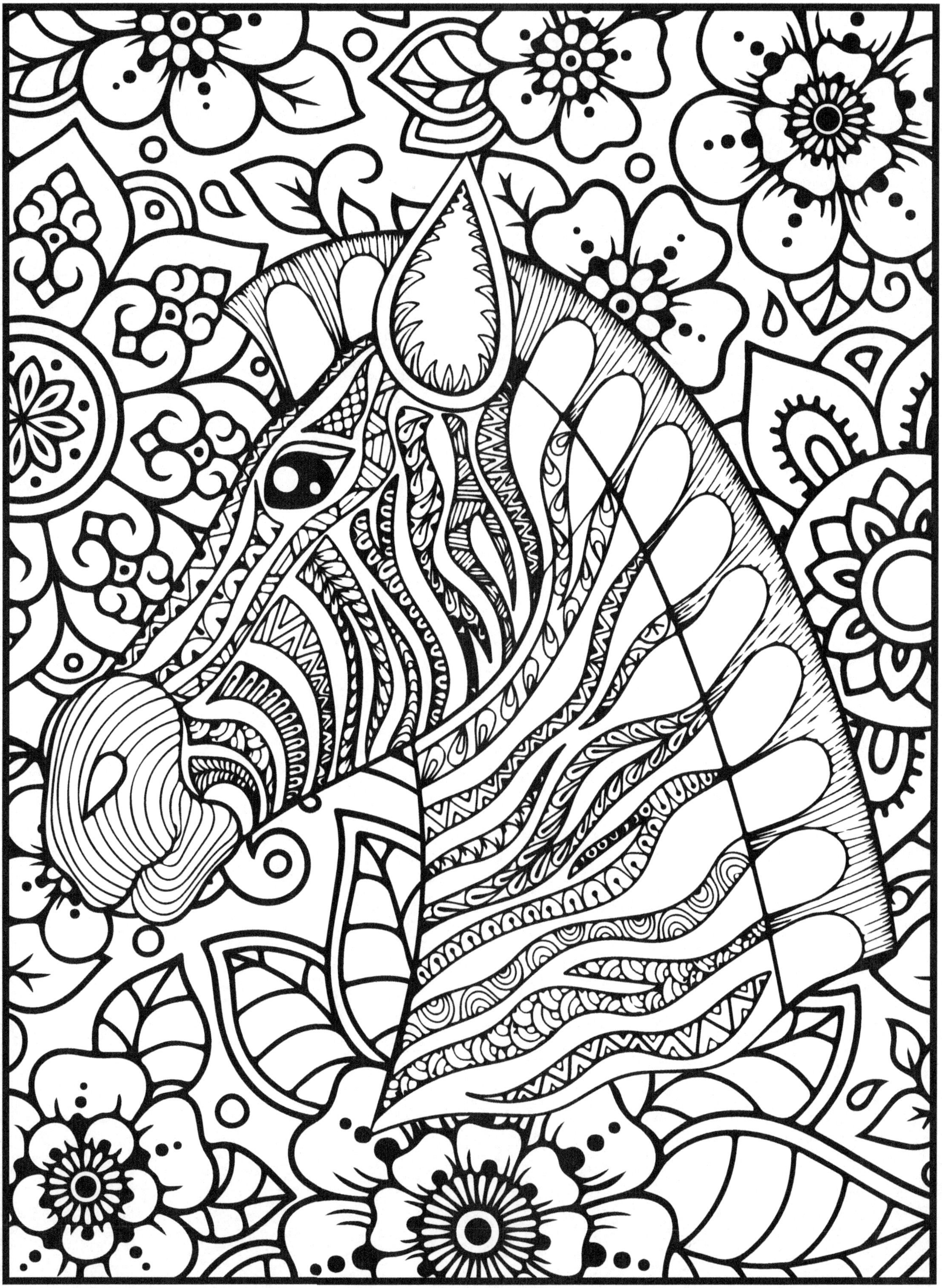

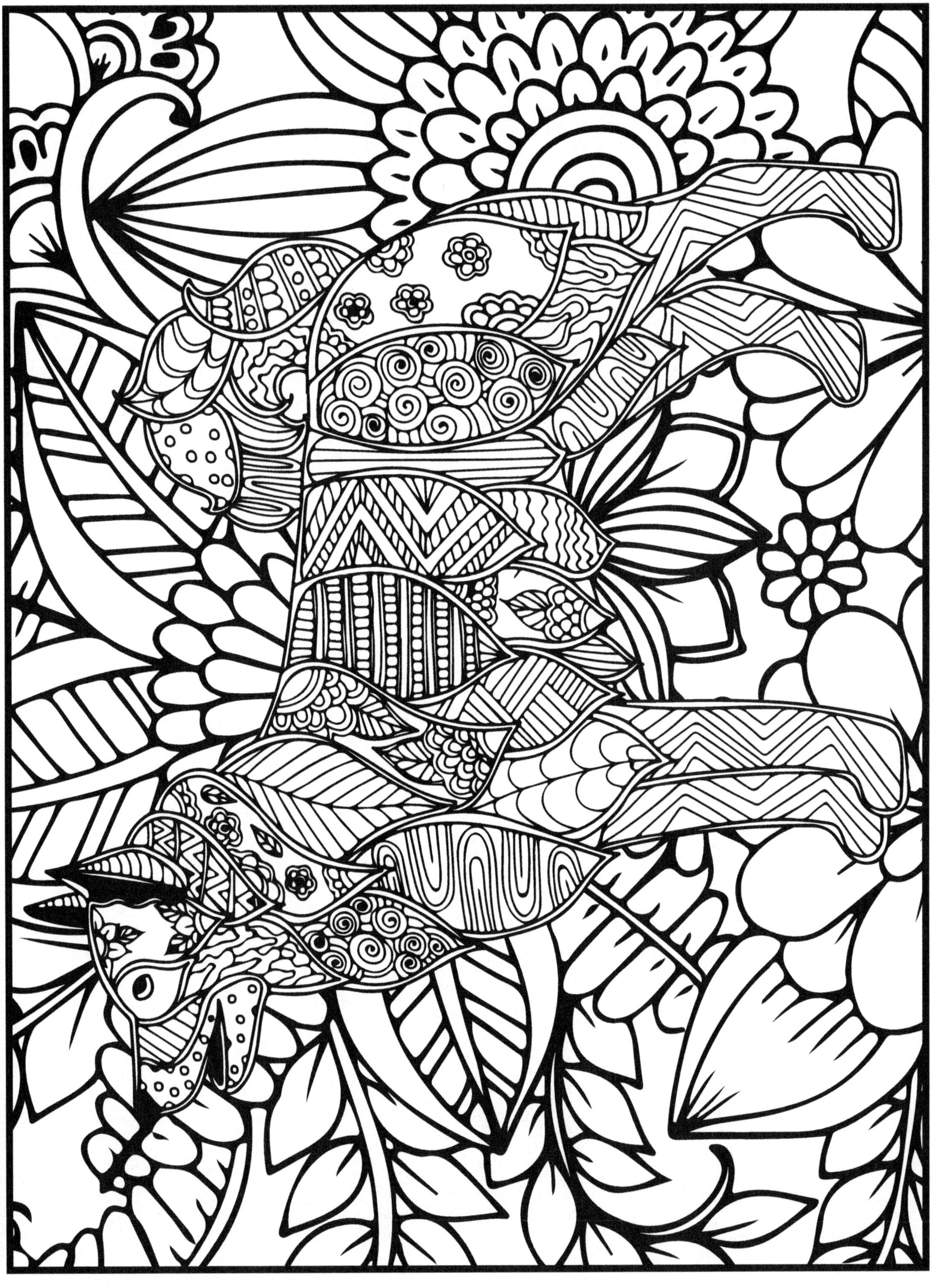

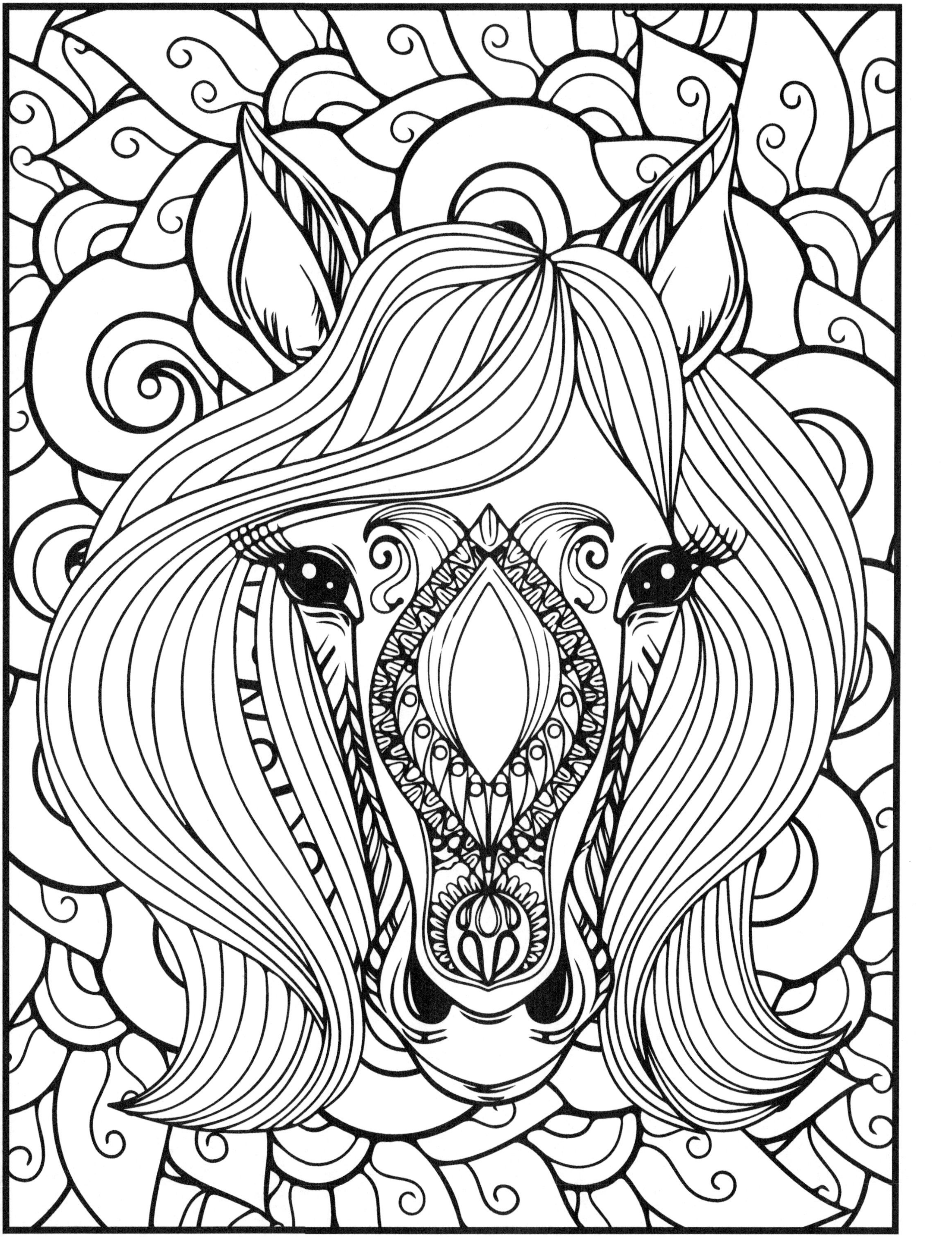

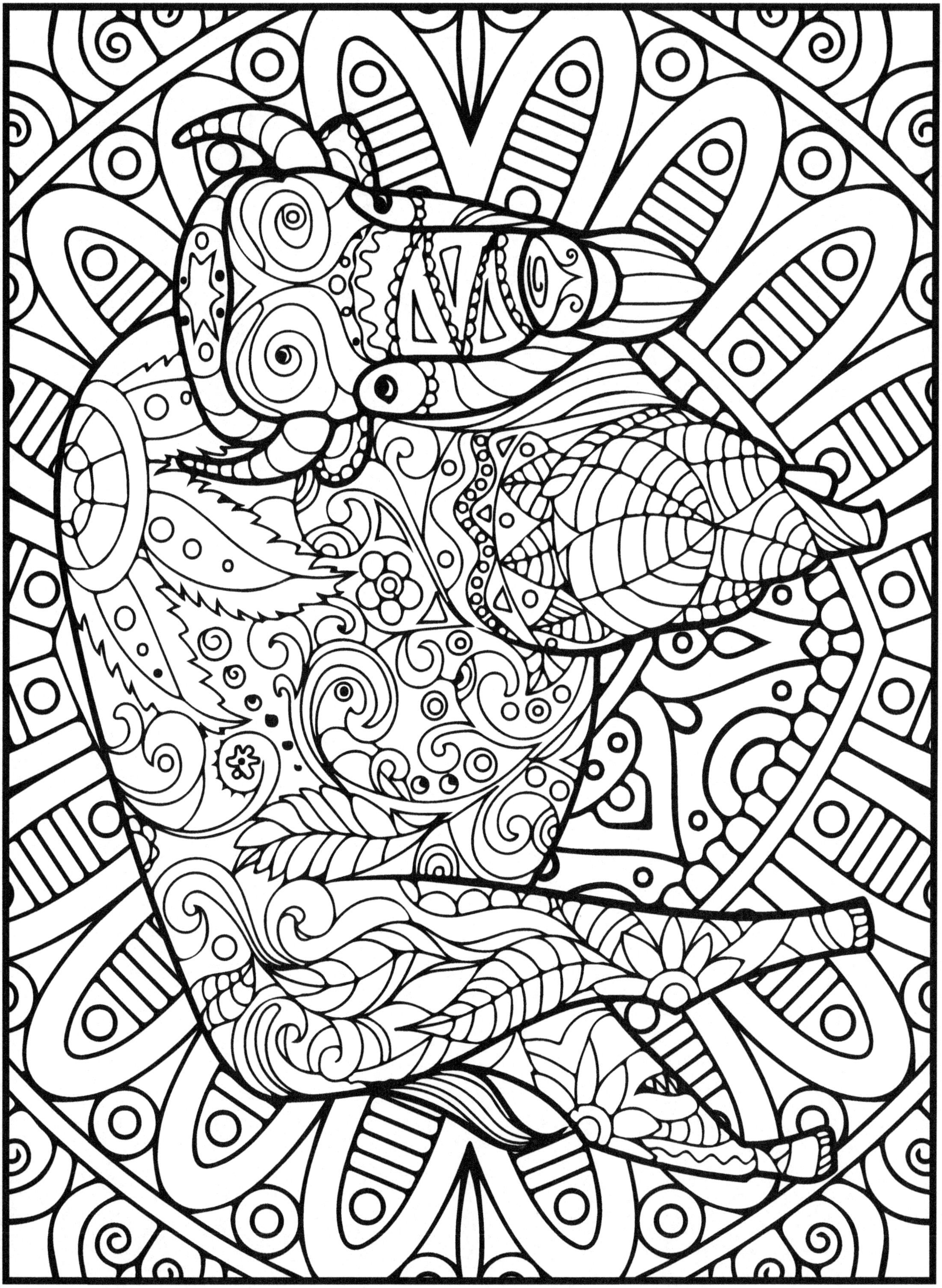

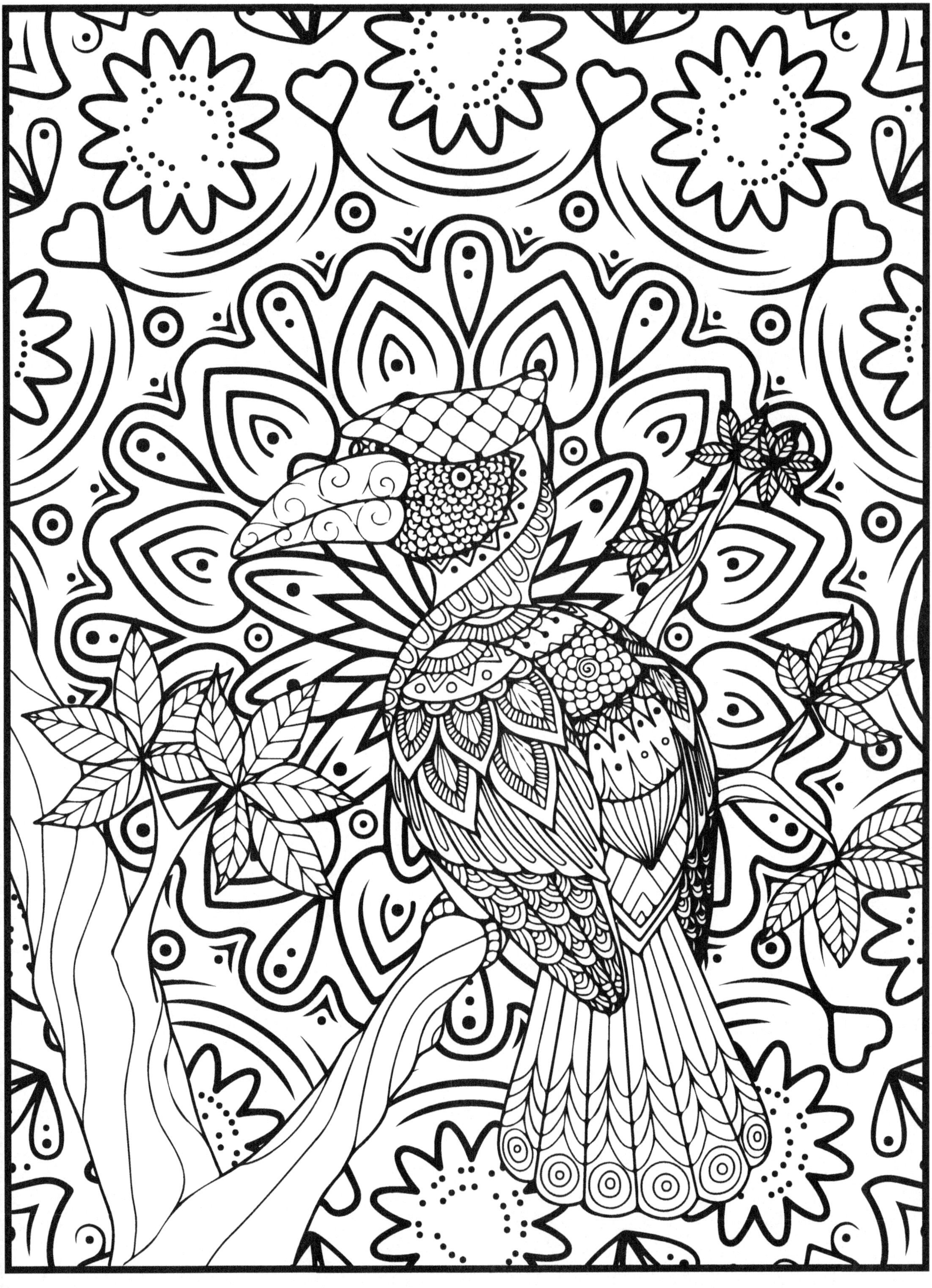

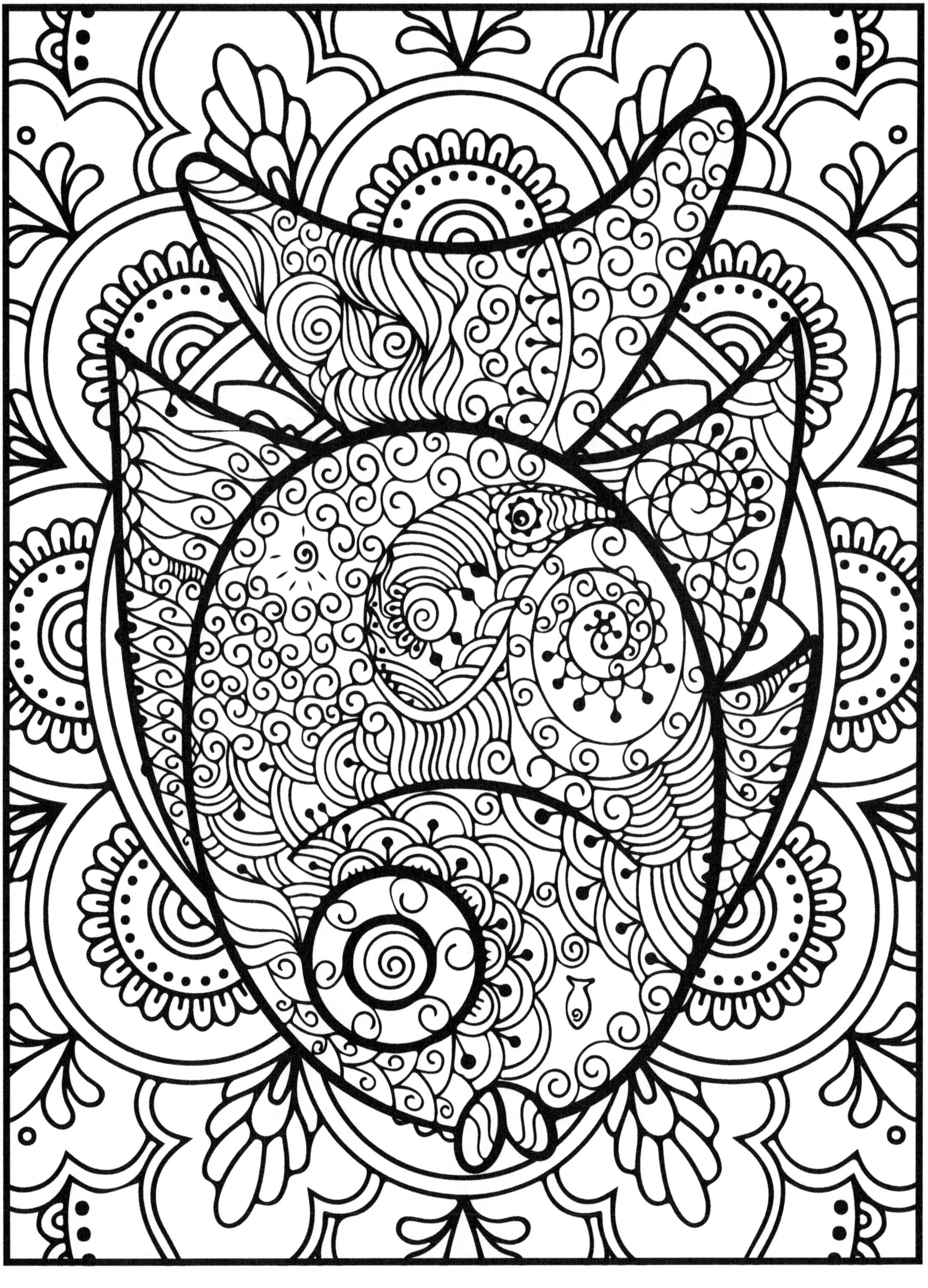

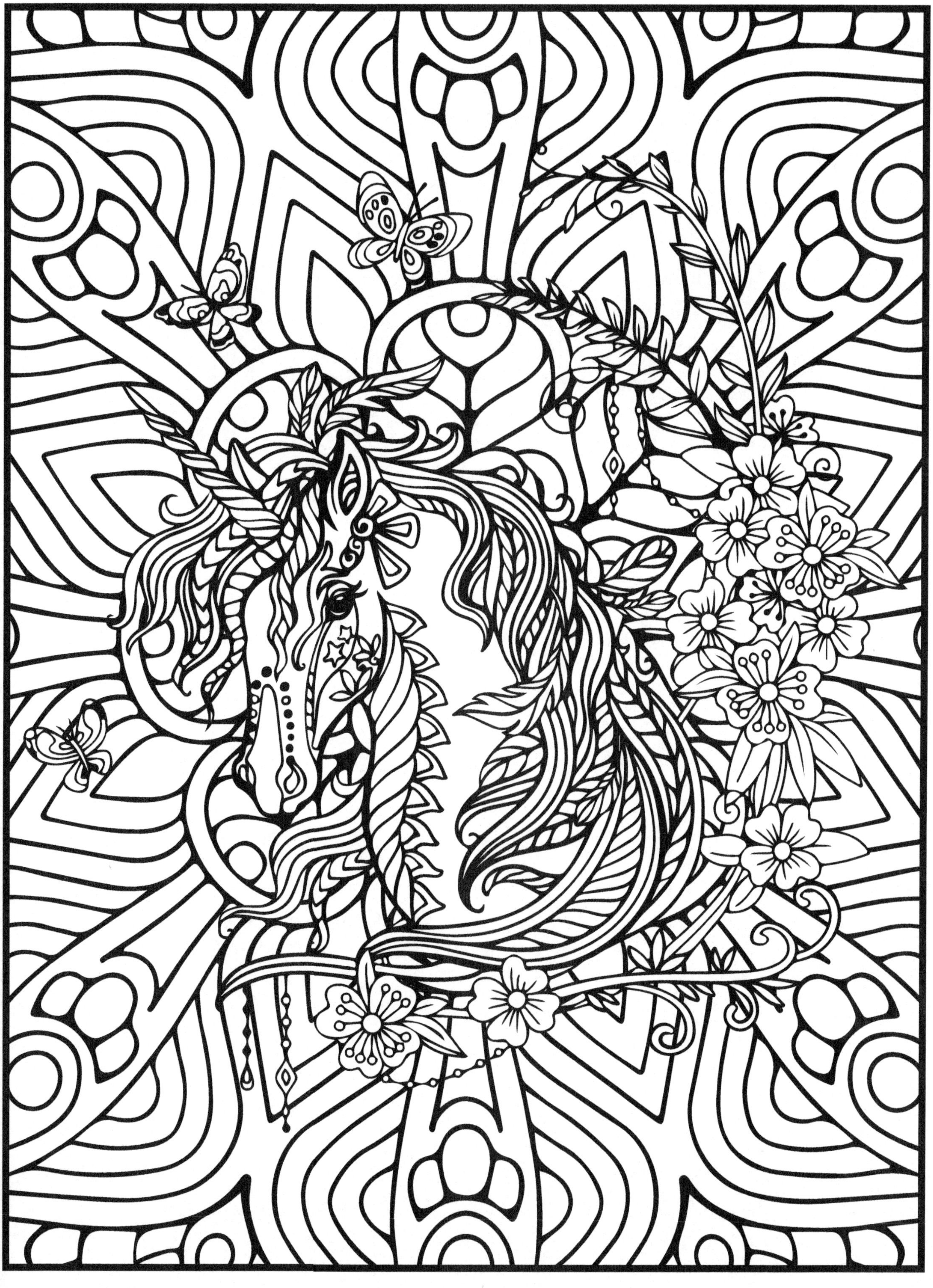

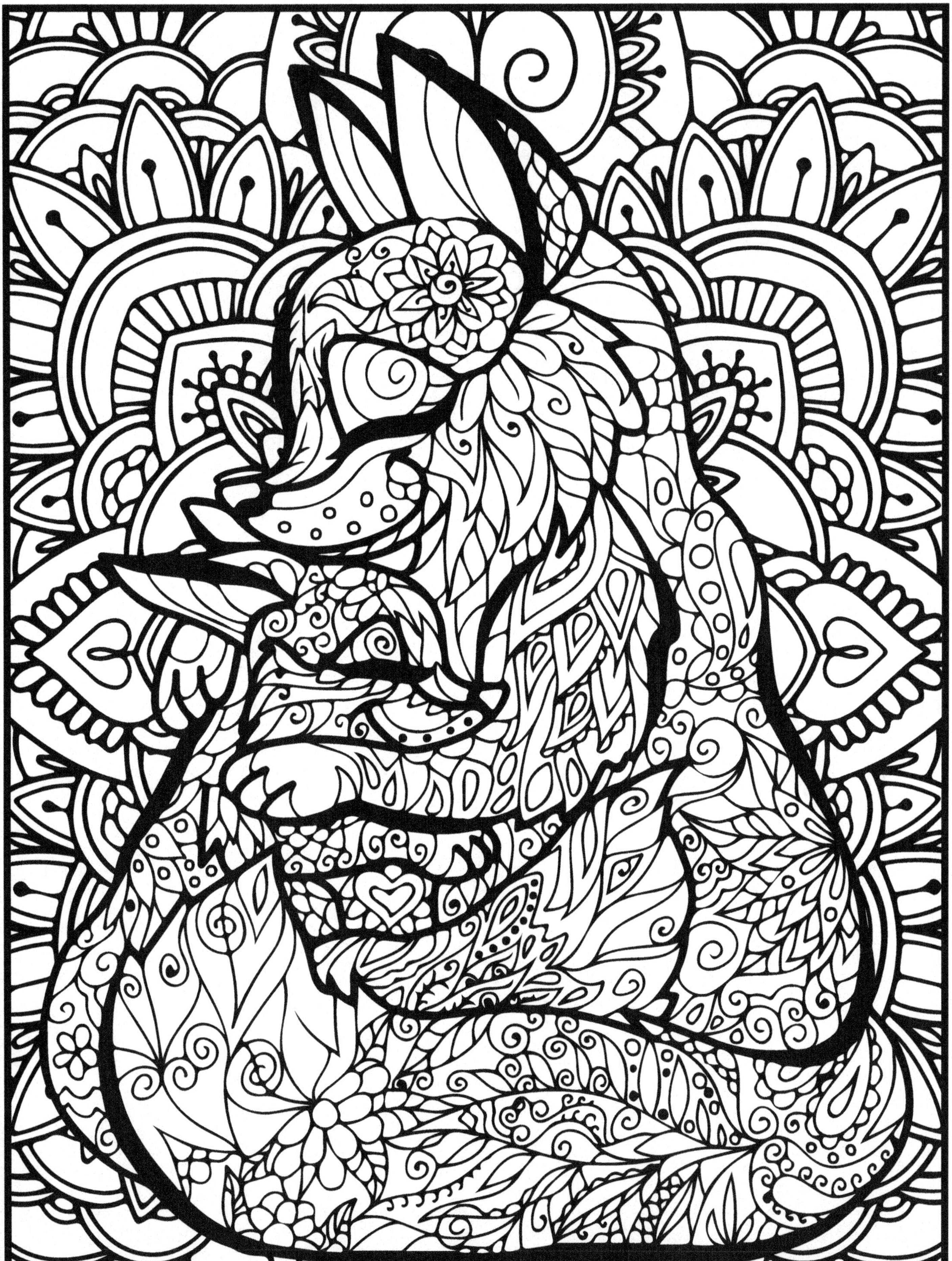

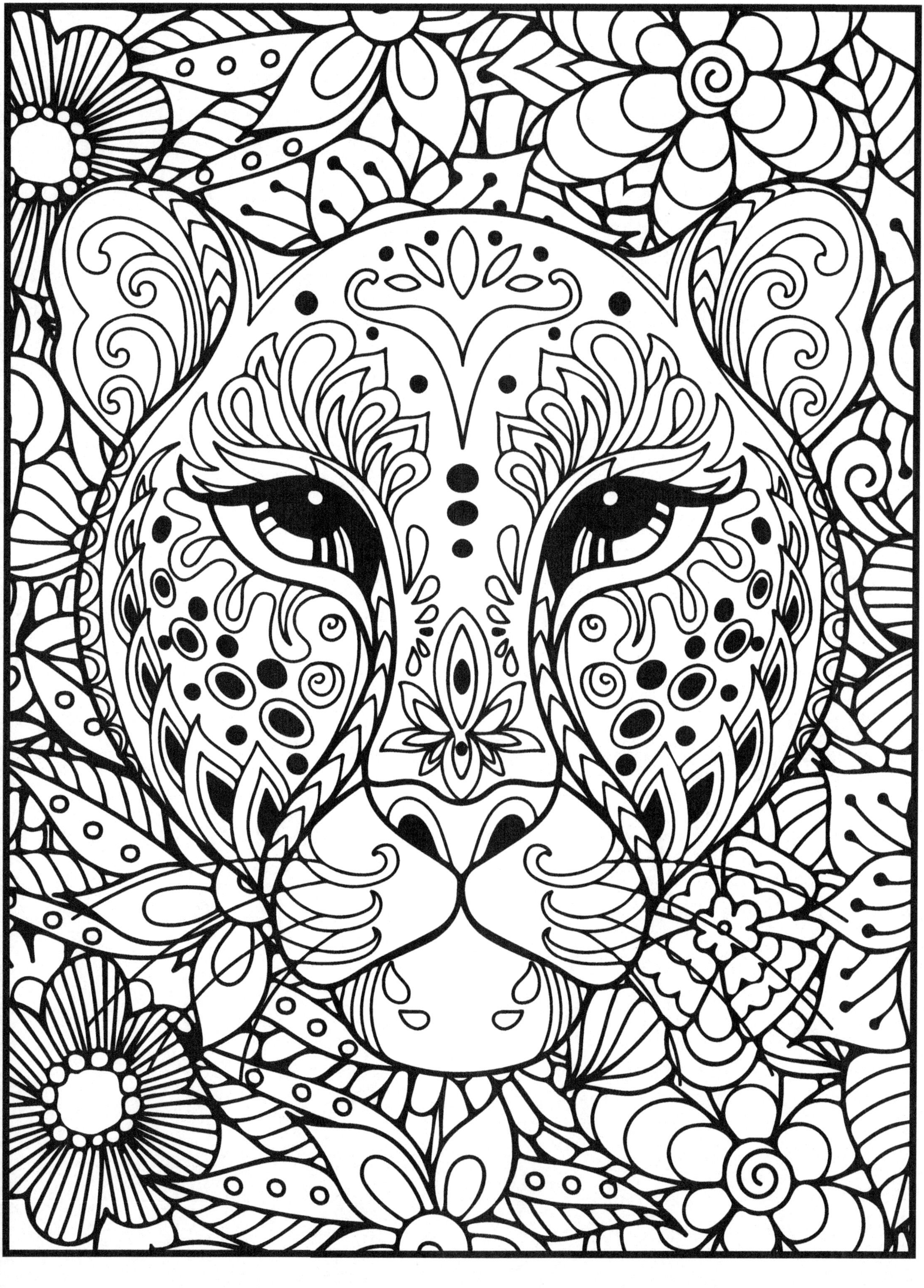

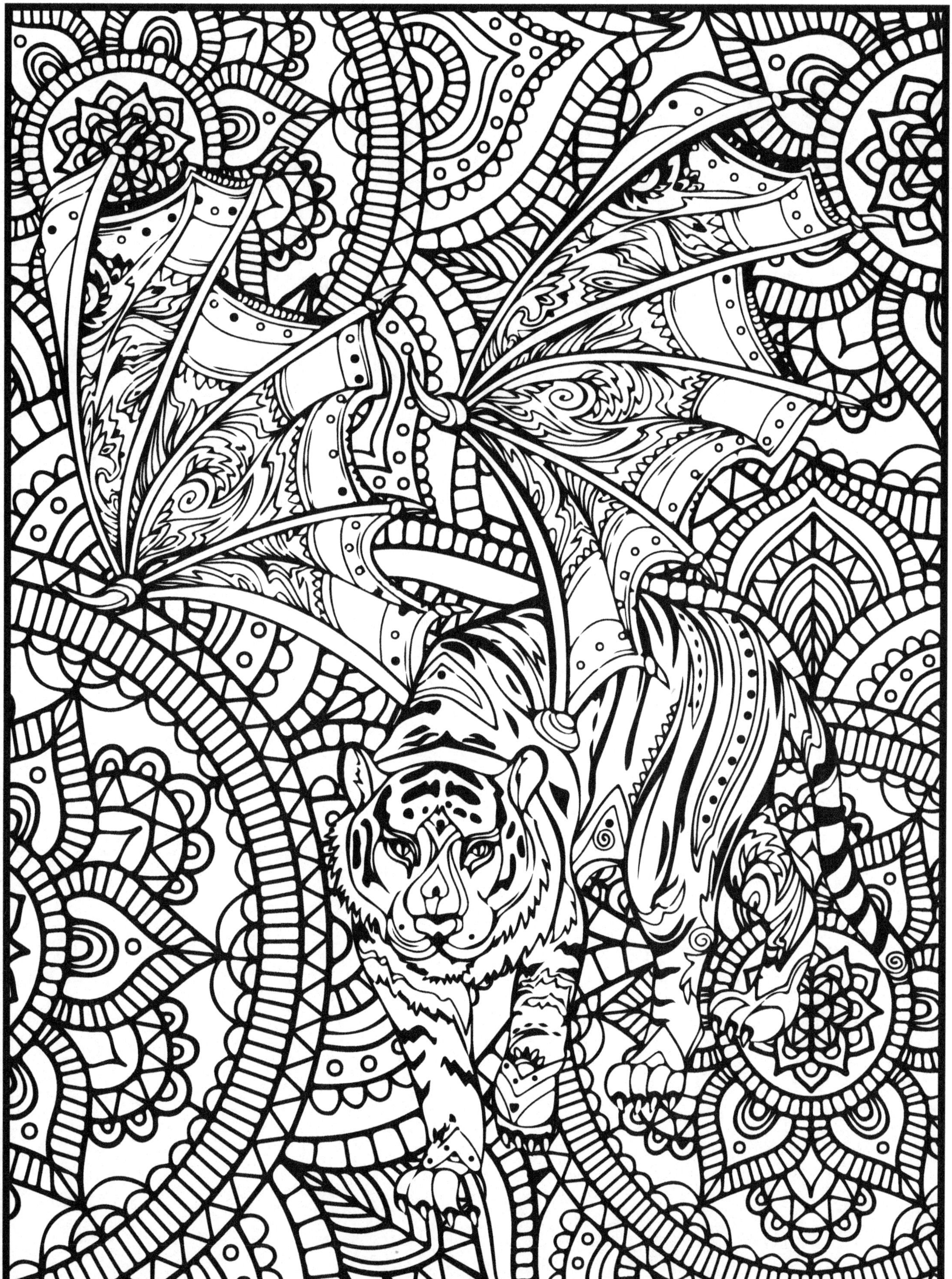

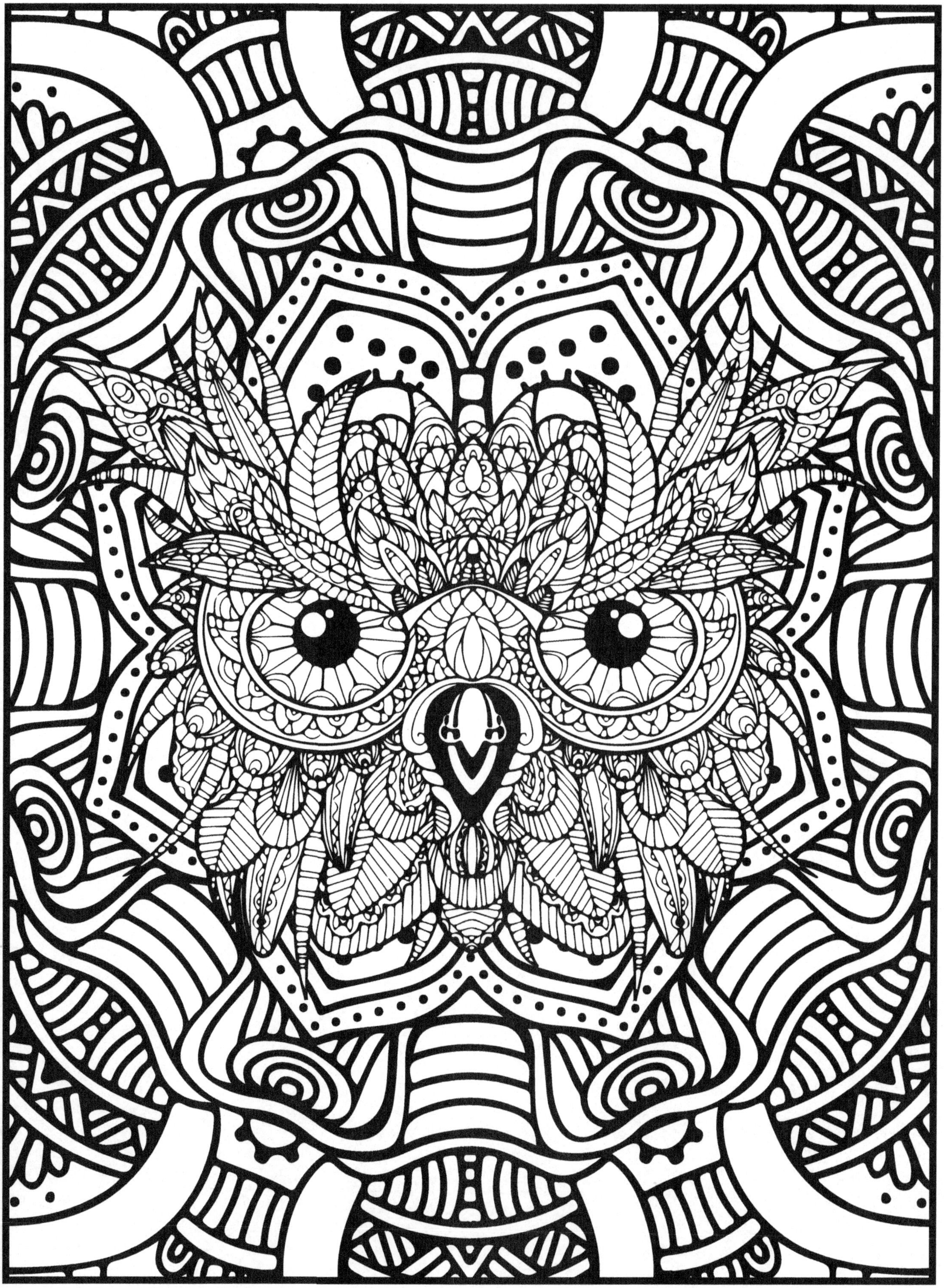

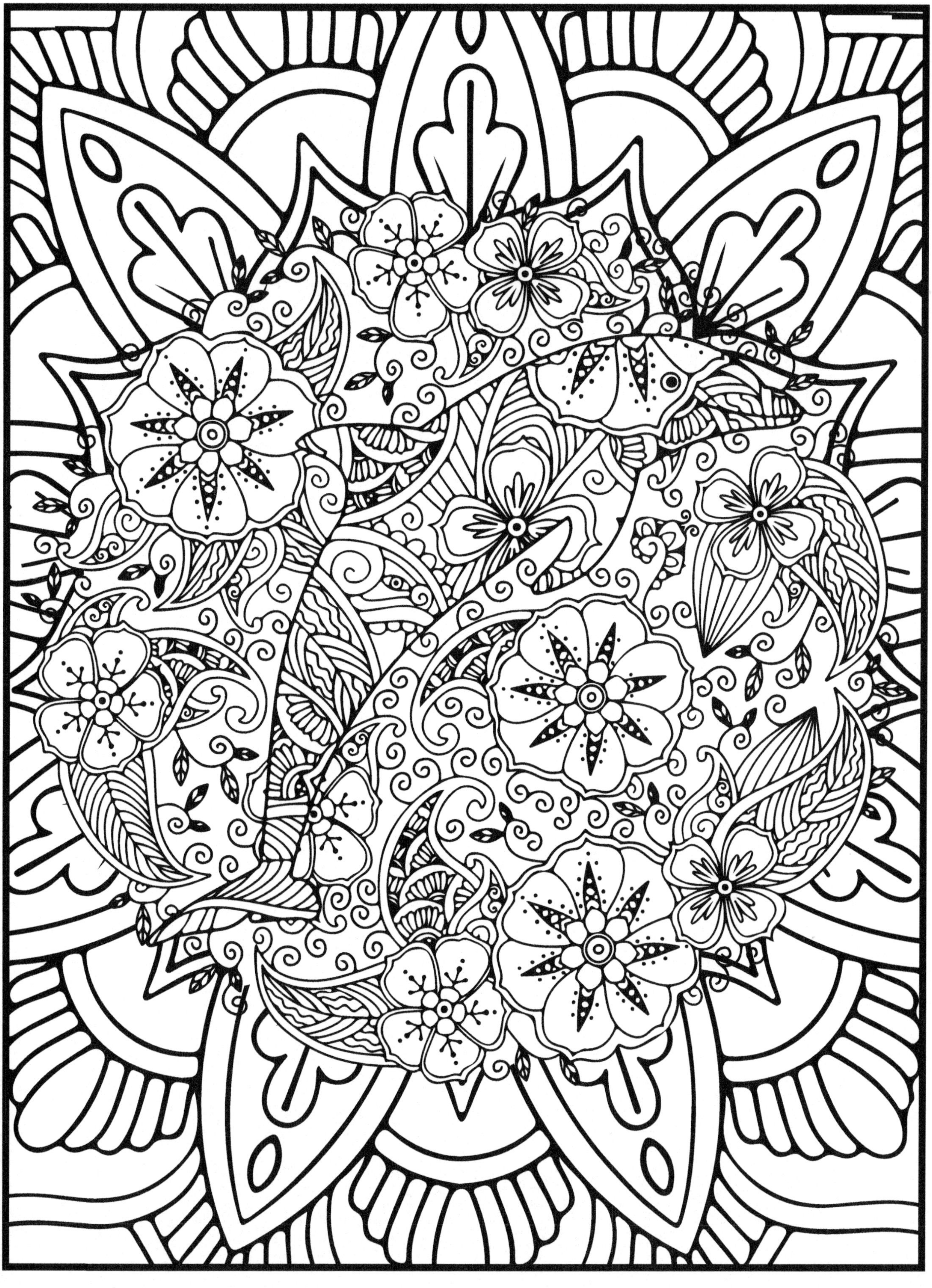

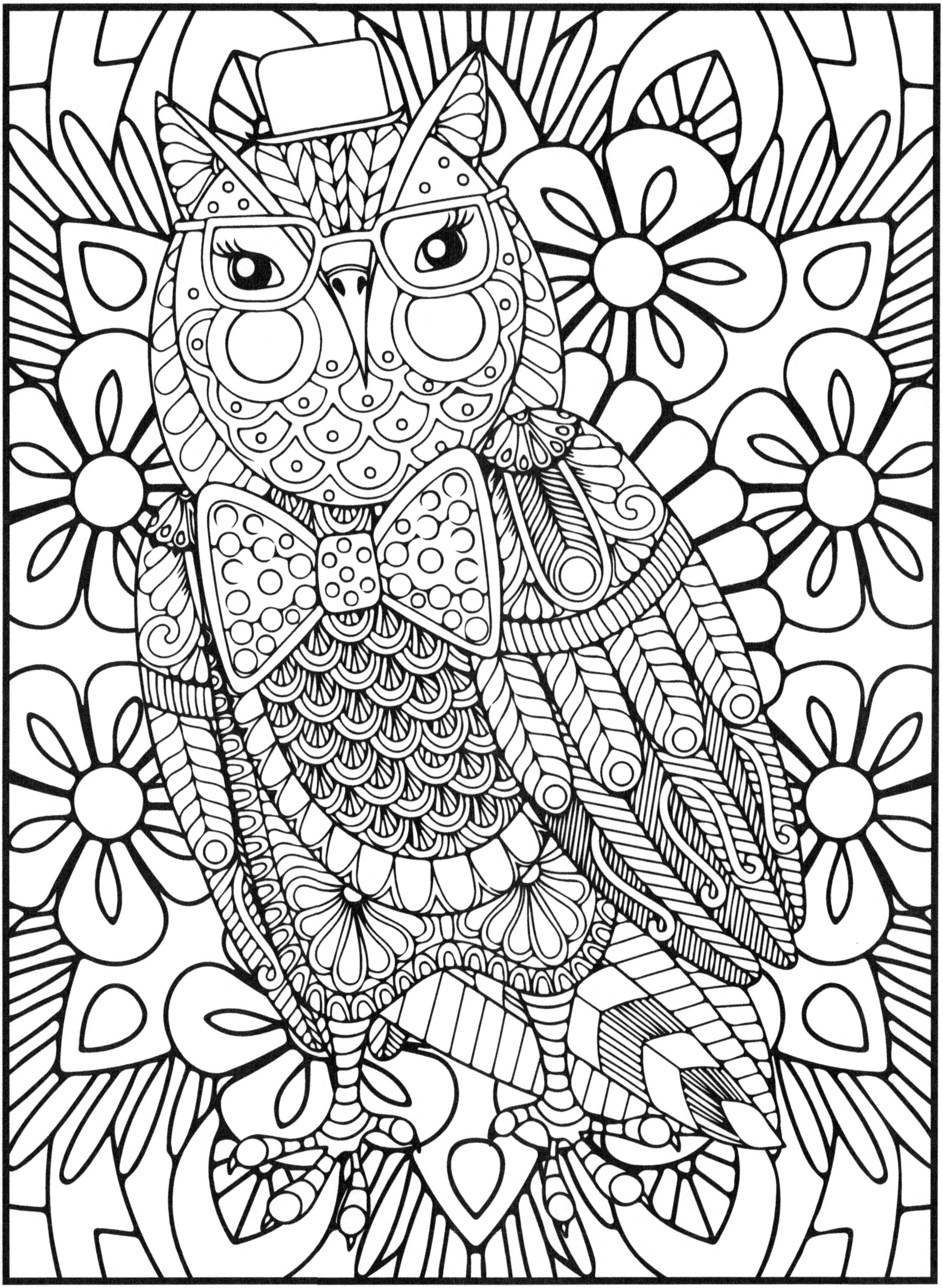

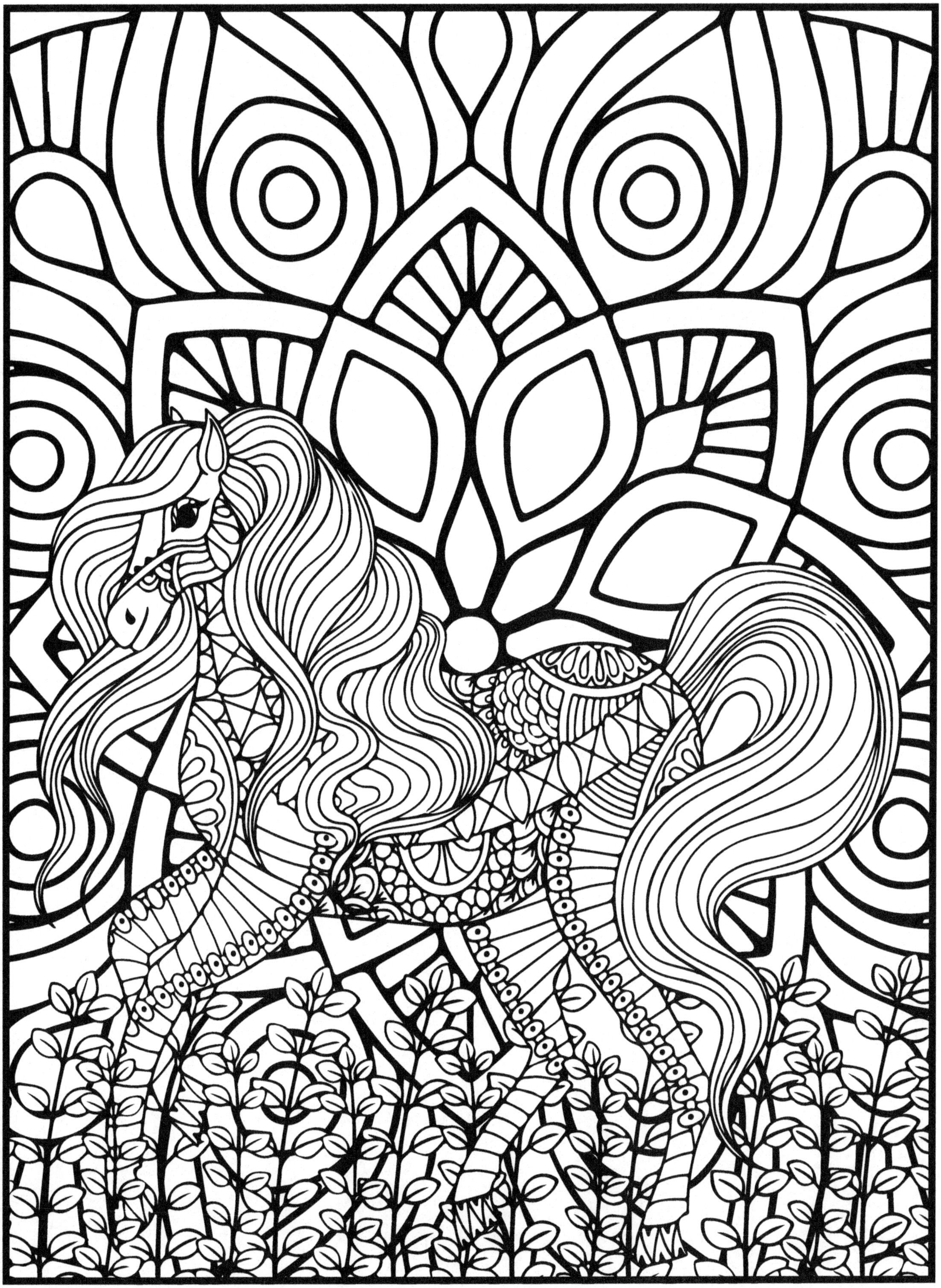

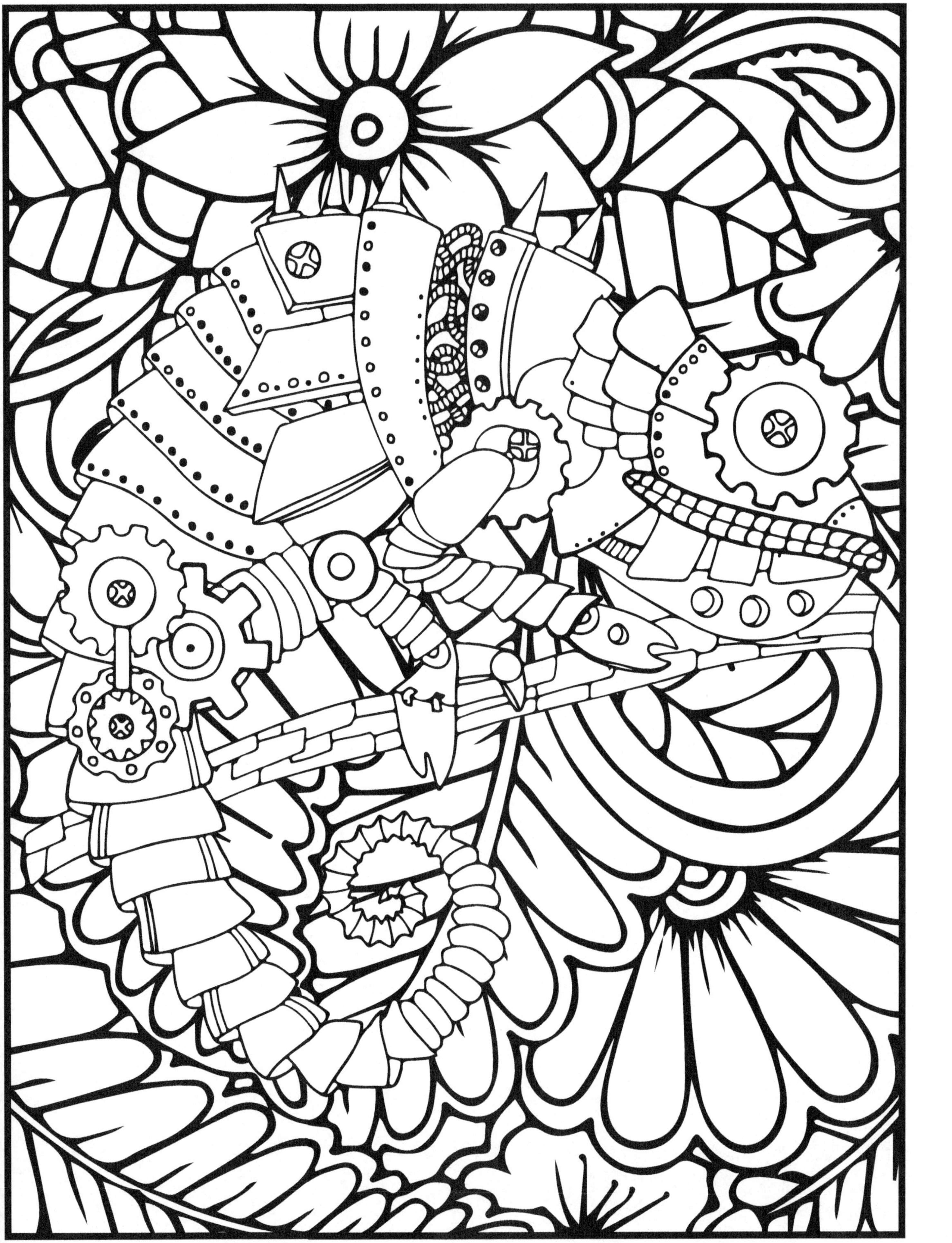

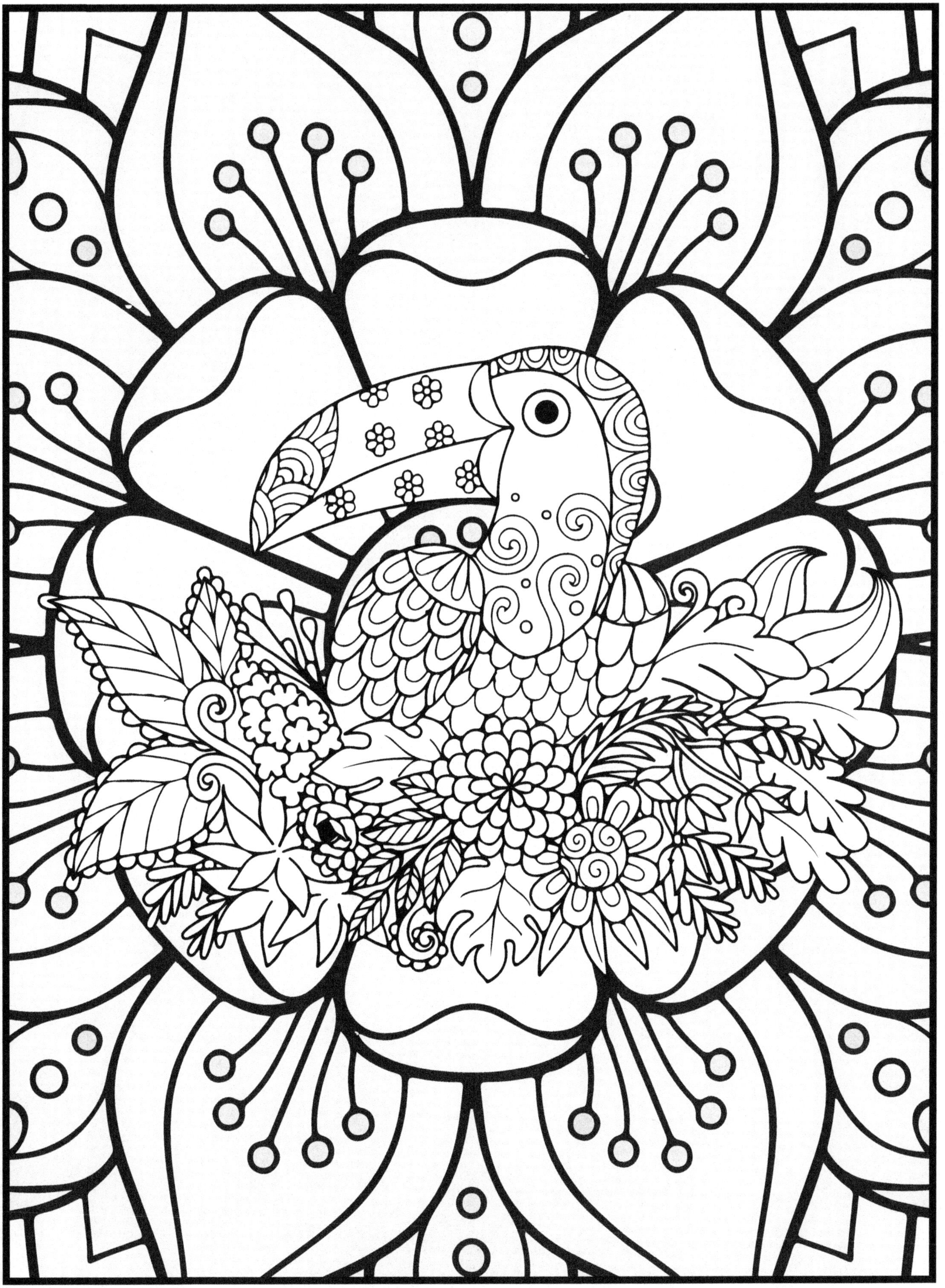

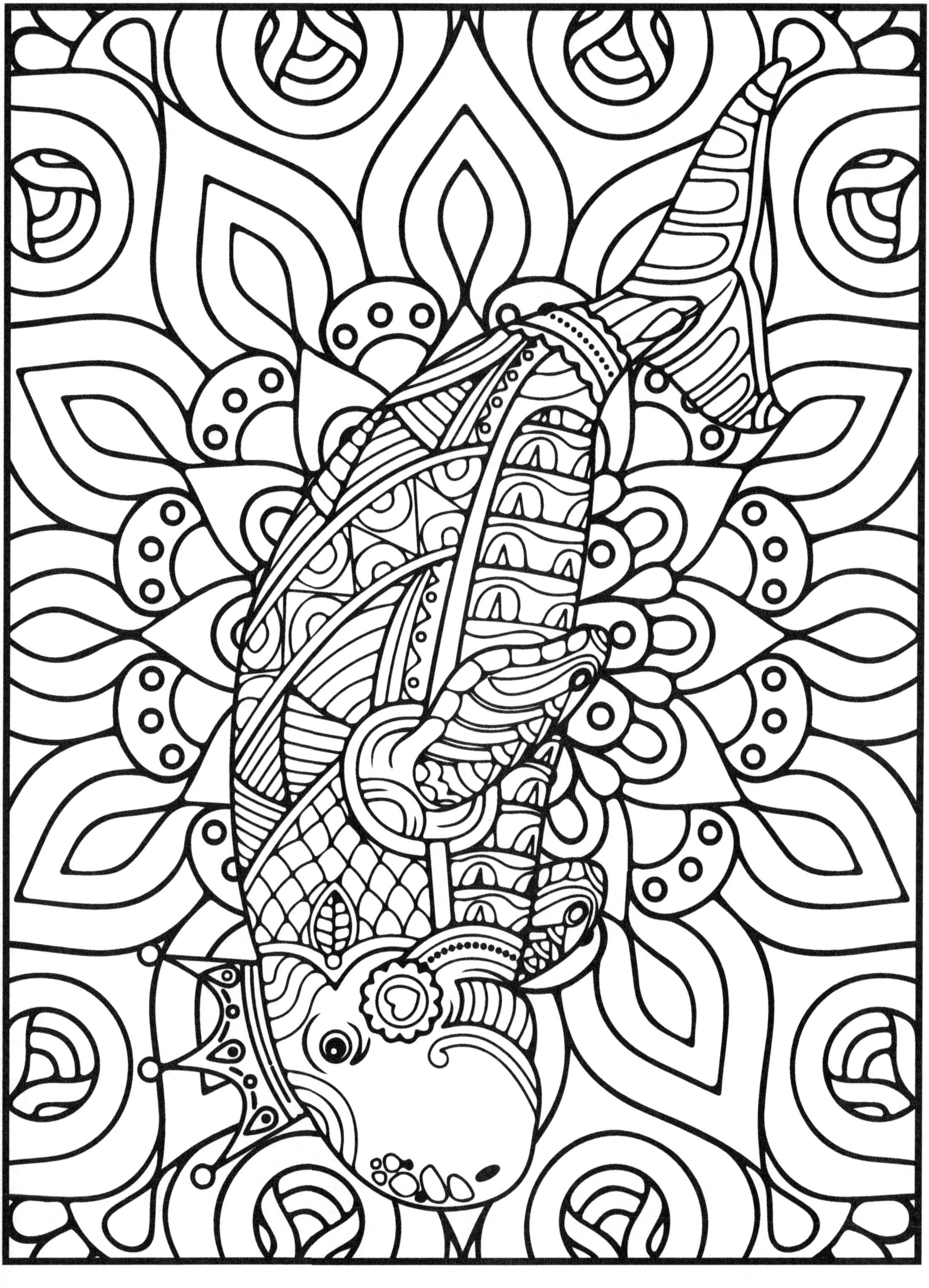

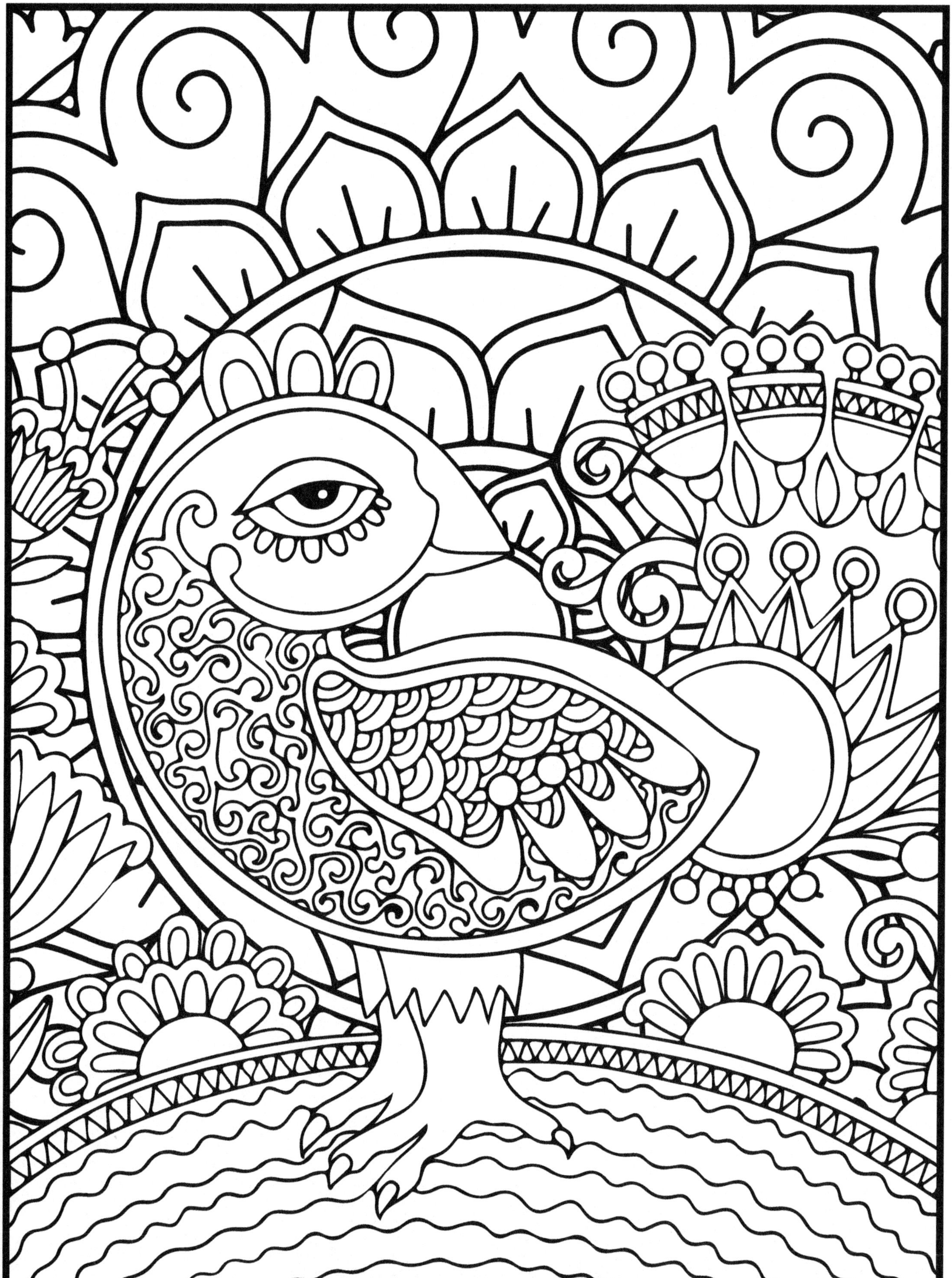

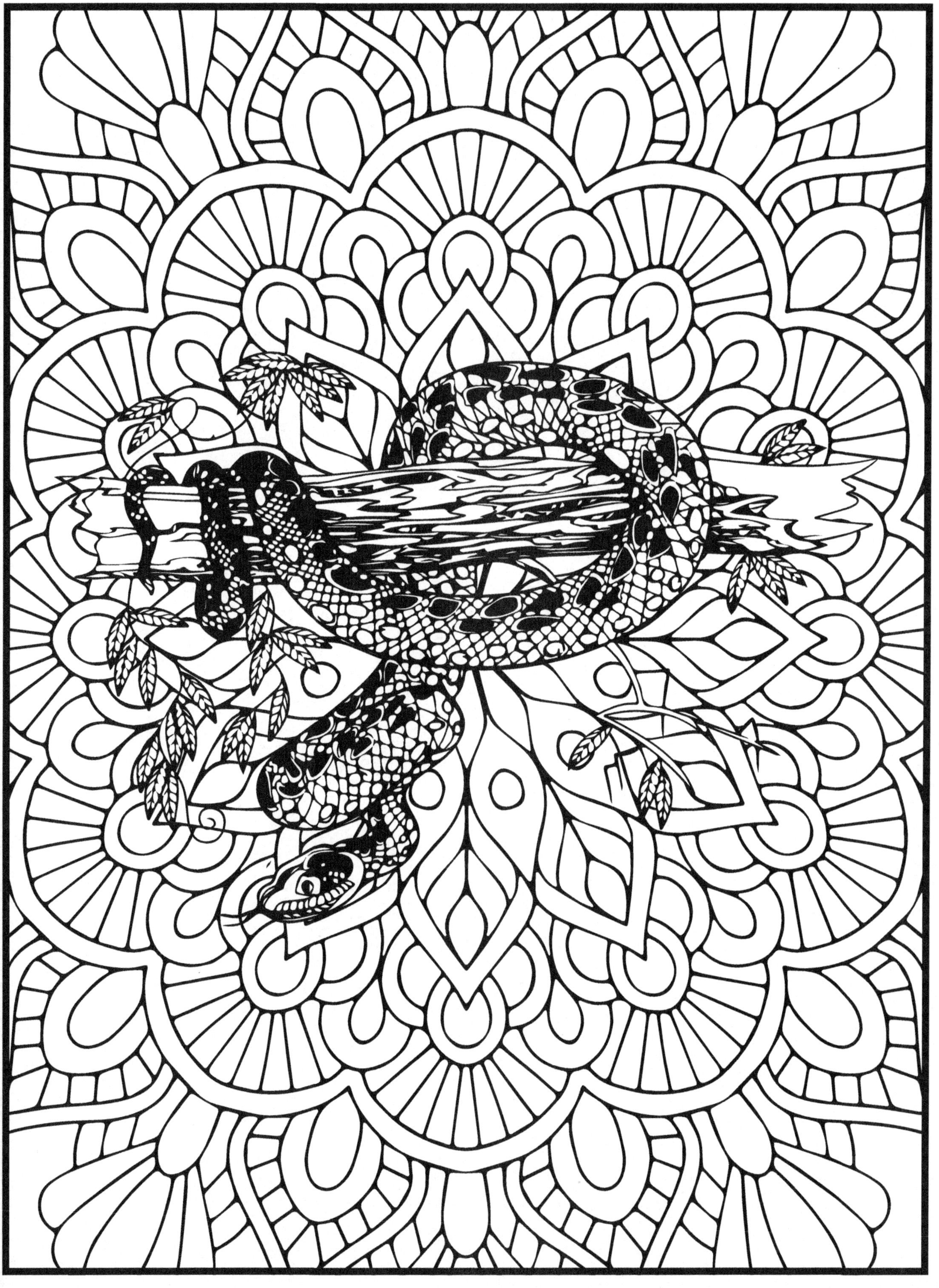

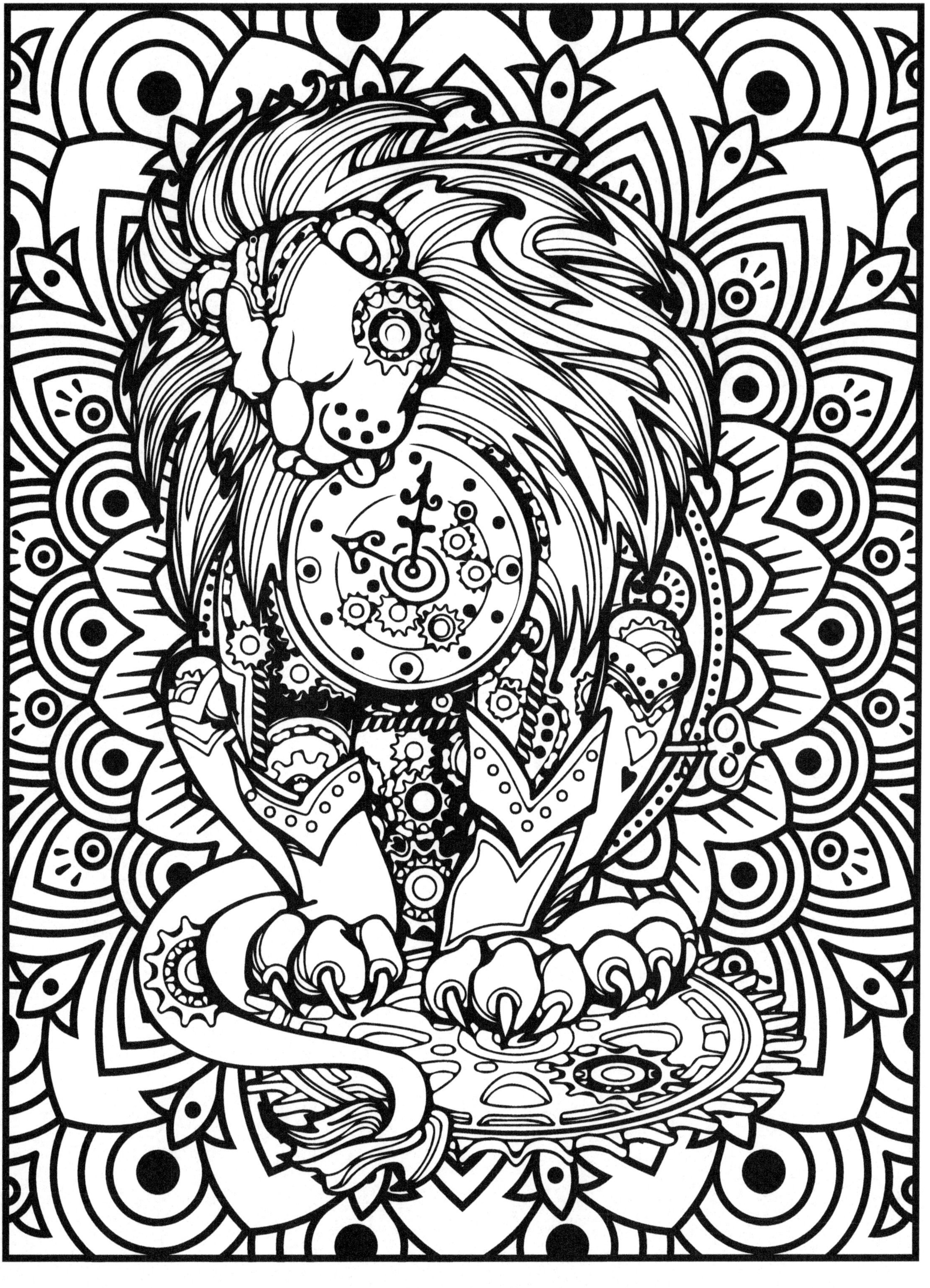

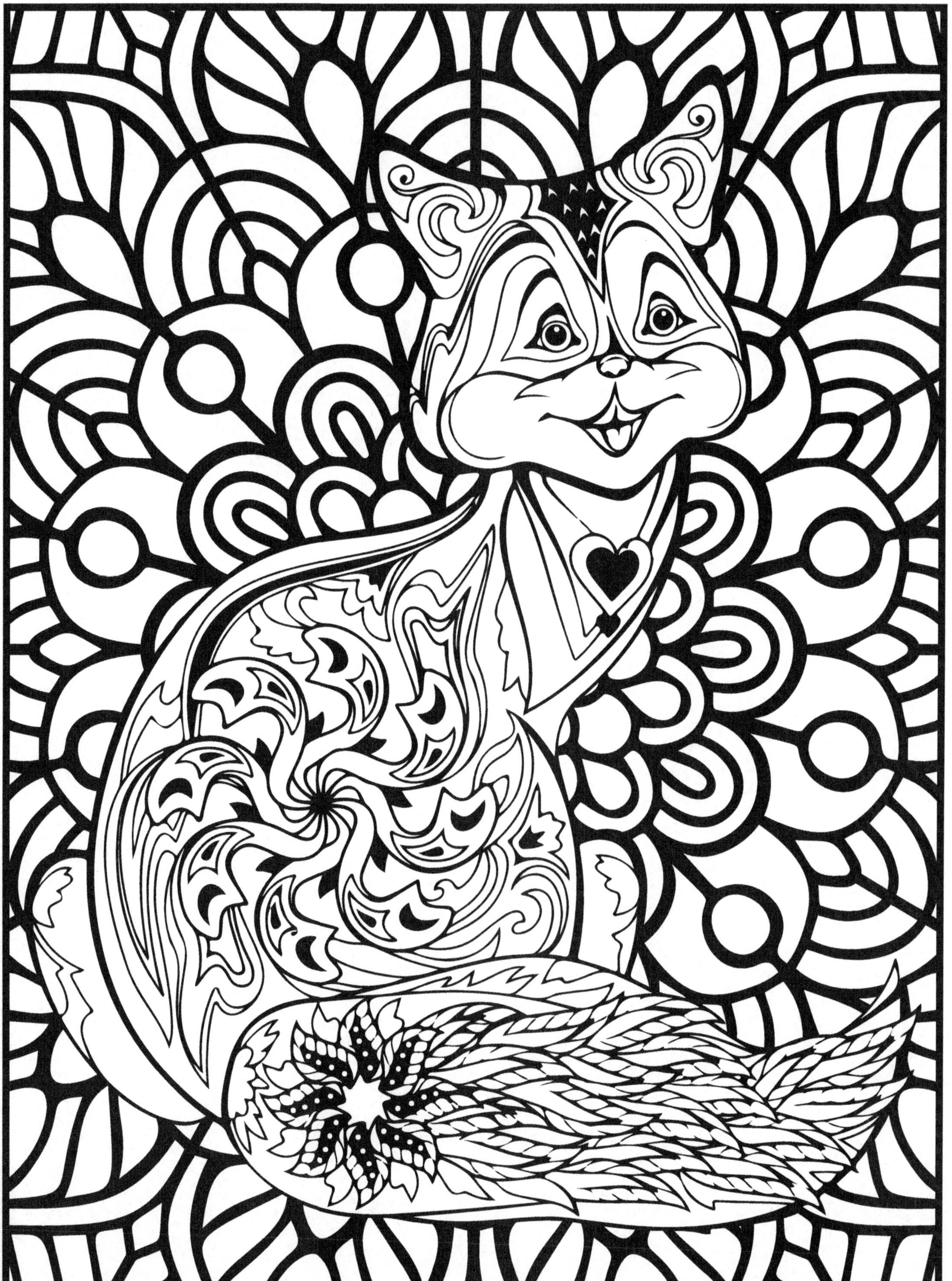

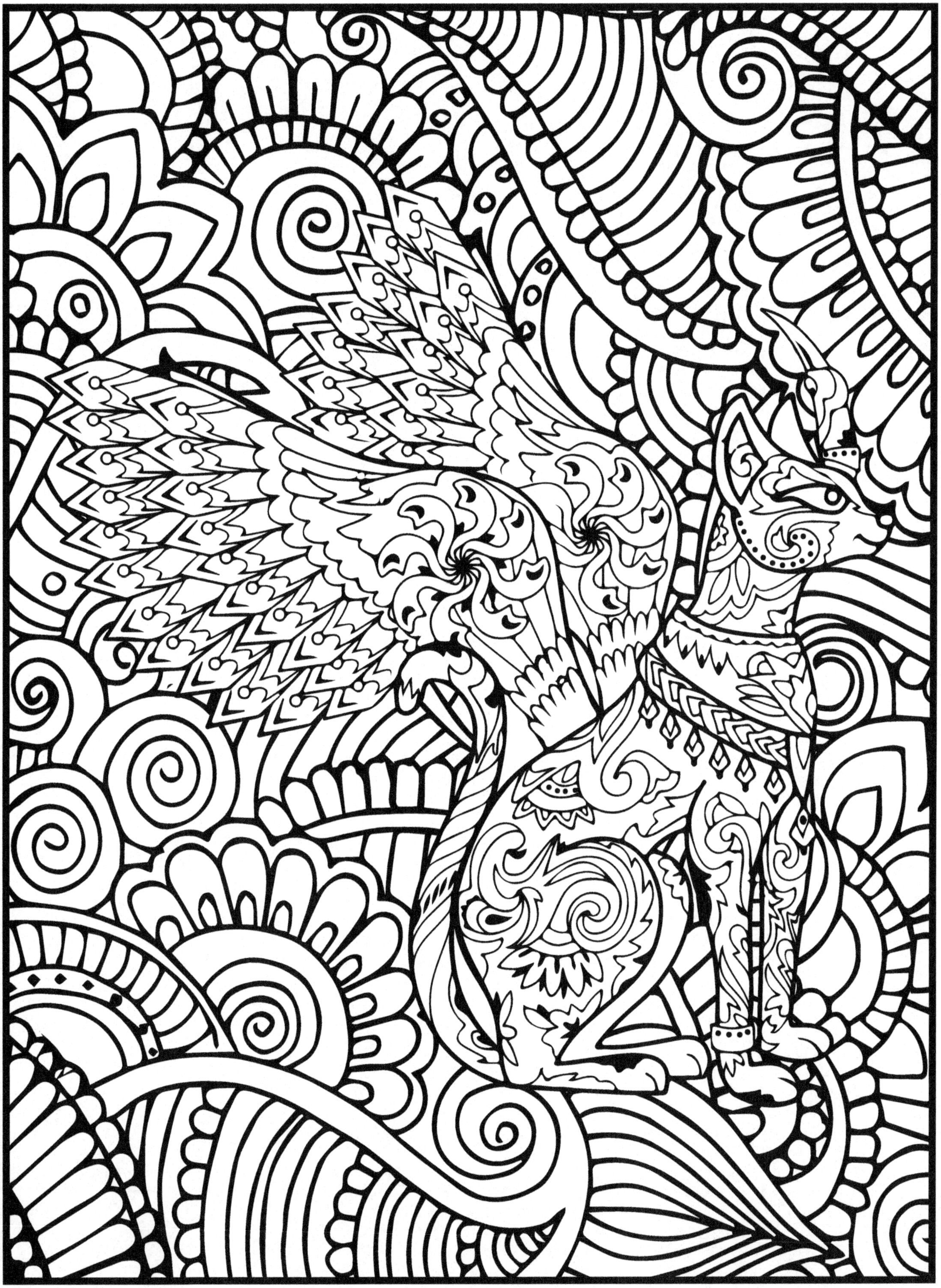

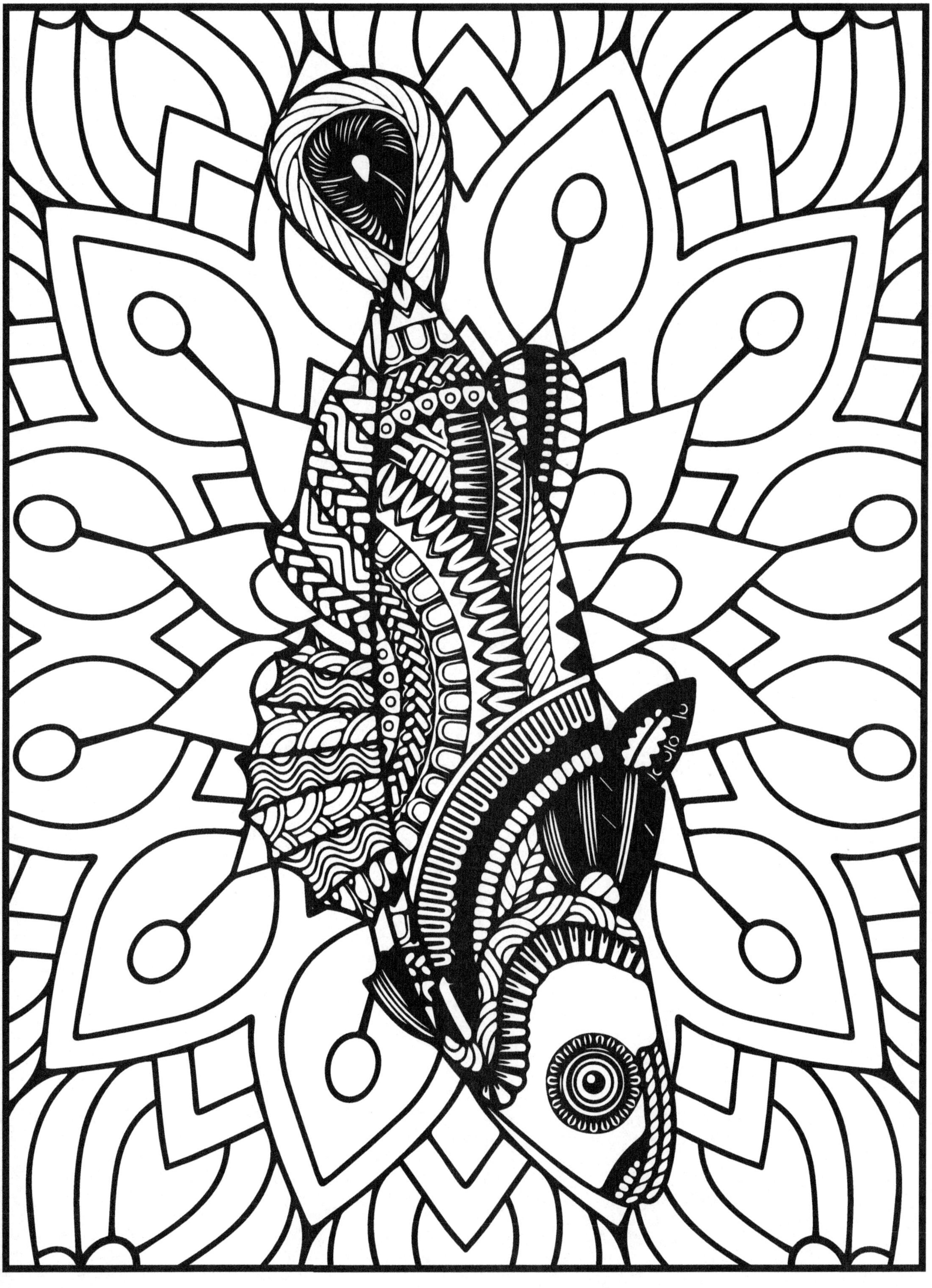

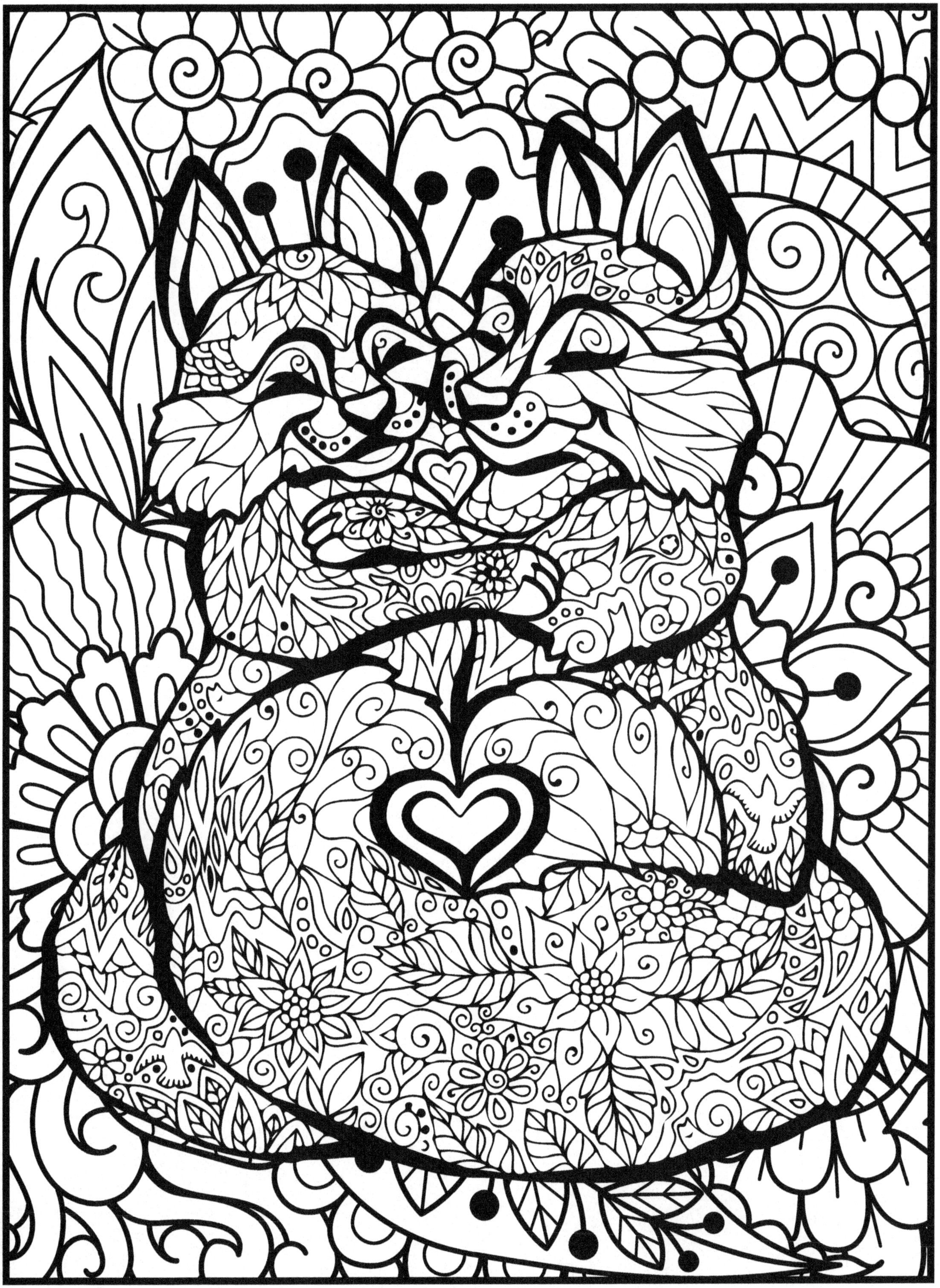

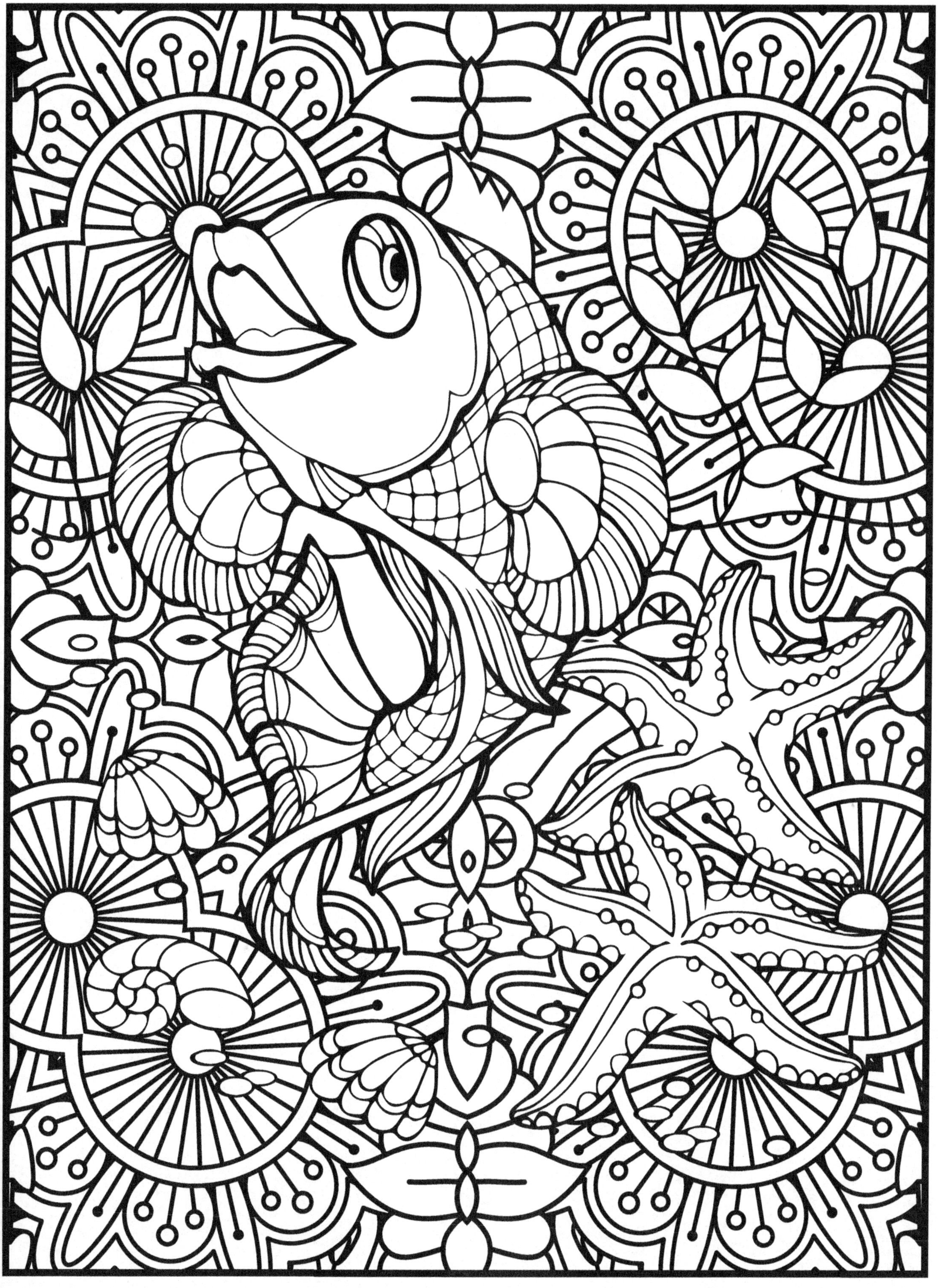

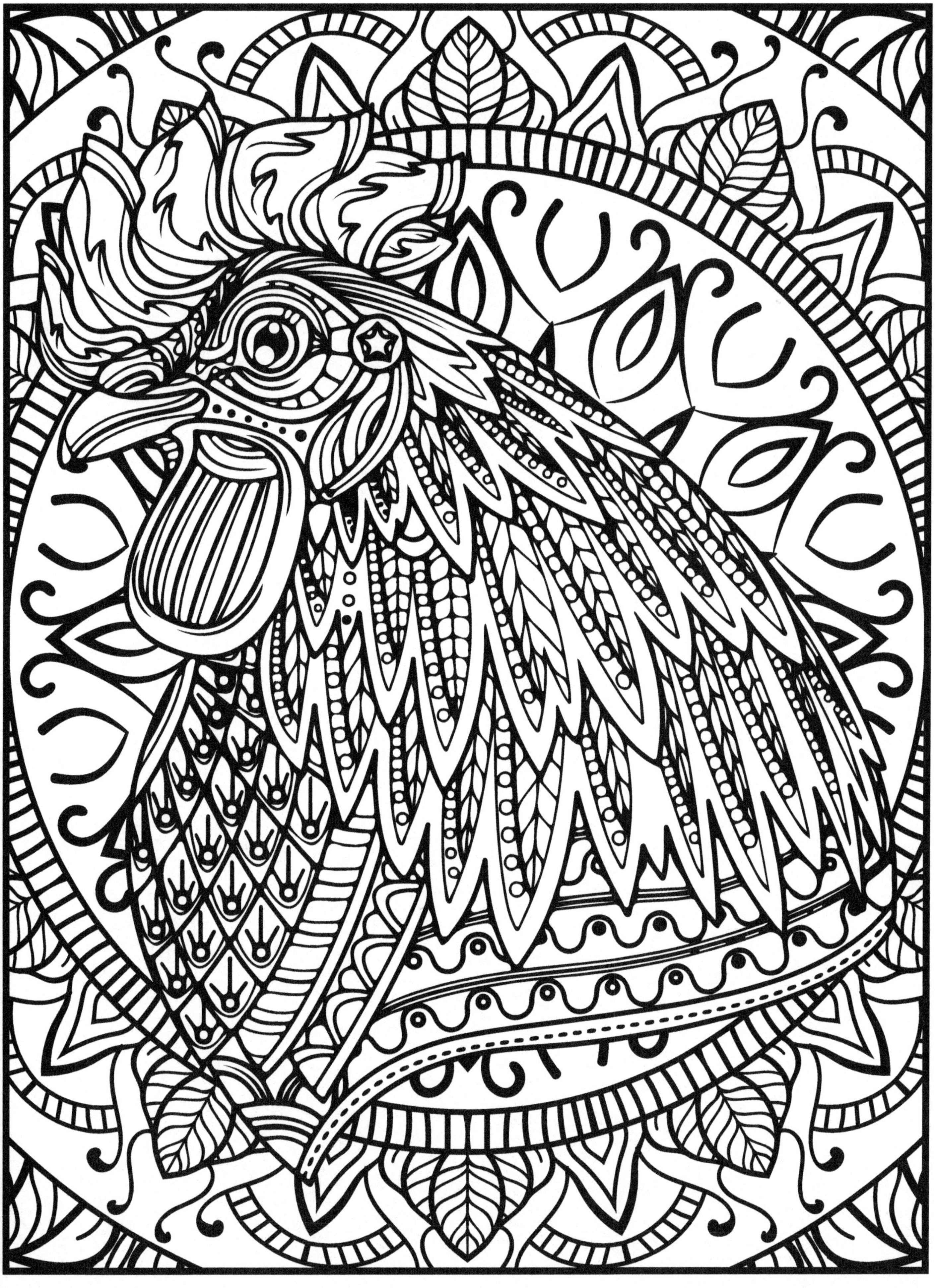

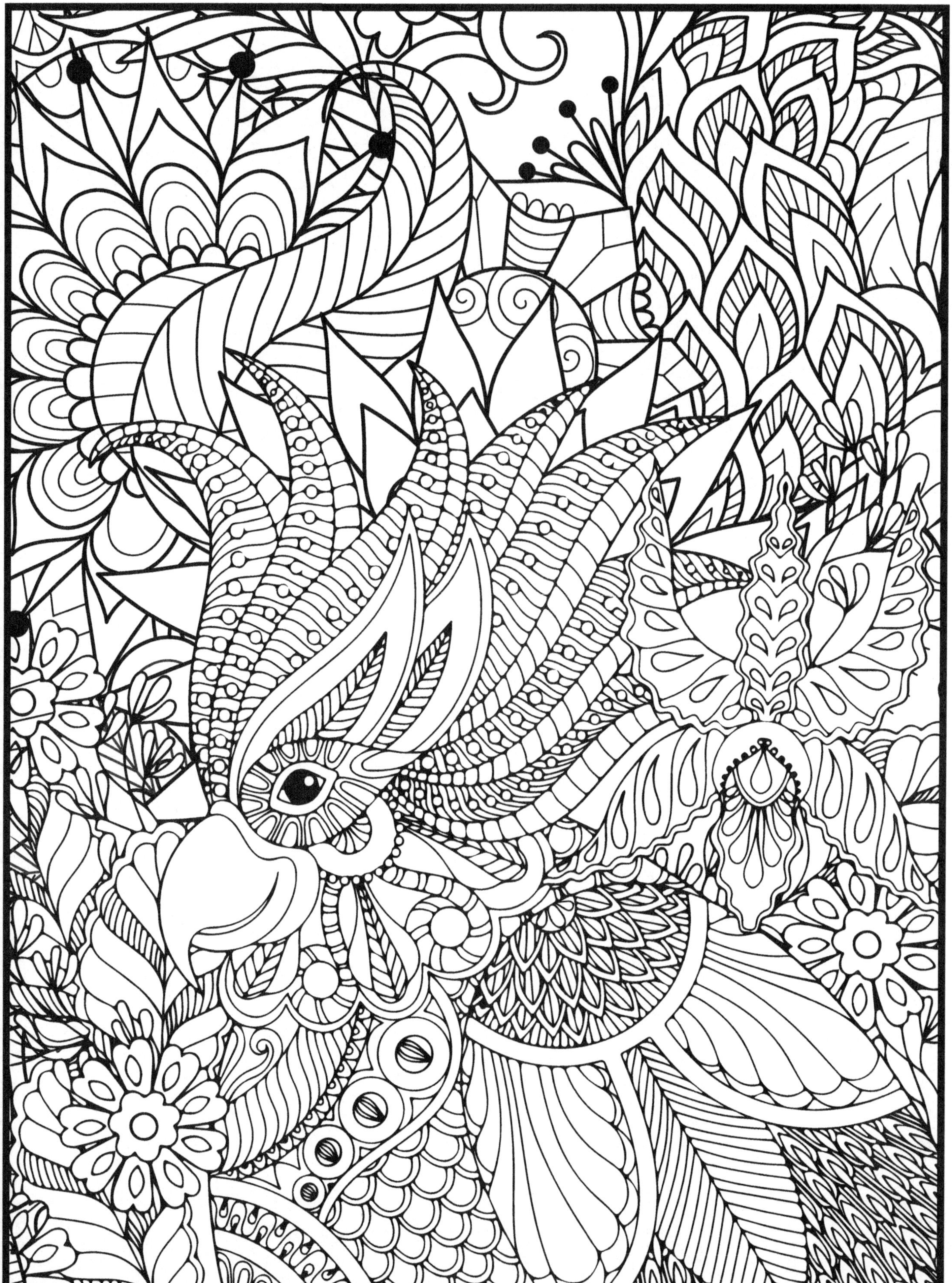

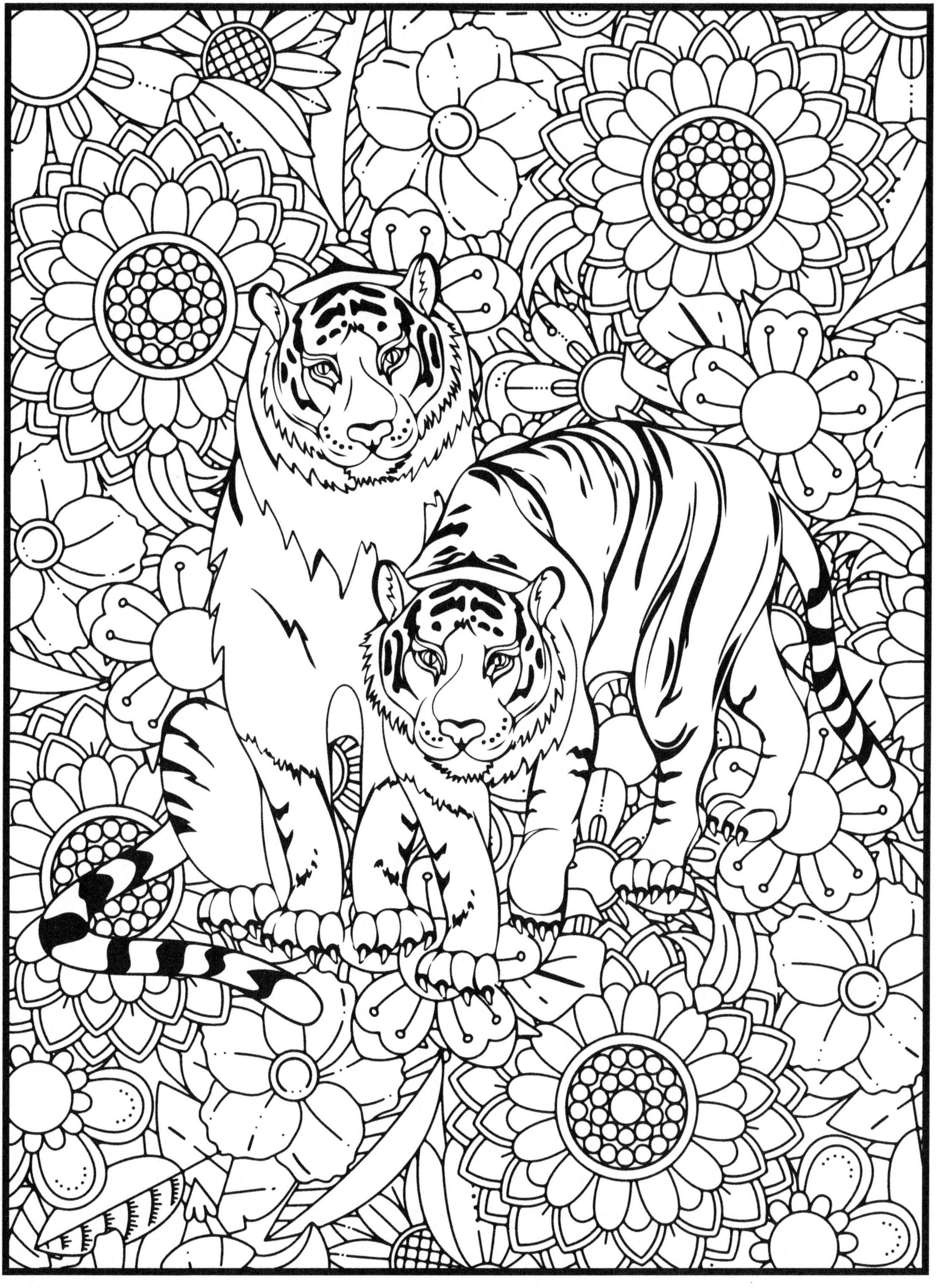

Like what you see?

Leave us a review!

Questions? Thoughts? We'd love to hear from you!

Printed in Great Britain
by Amazon

23791826R00059